The Light Bringer

Some more books of White Eagle's teaching

A WAKENING: A GUIDE FOR LIVING WITH DEATH & DYING

BEAUTIFUL ROAD HOME

THE BOOK OF STAR LIGHT

THE GENTLE BROTHER

GOLDEN HARVEST

HEAL THYSELF

JESUS TEACHER AND HEALER

THE LIVING WORD OF ST JOHN

MORNING LIGHT

PRAYER IN THE NEW AGE

THE PATH OF THE SOUL

THE QUIET MIND

SPIRITUAL UNFOLDMENT 1

SPIRITUAL UNFOLDMENT 2

SPIRITUAL UNFOLDMENT 3

SPIRITUAL UNFOLDMENT 4

THE SOURCE OF ALL OUR STRENGTH

THE STILL VOICE

SUNRISE

WALKING WITH THE ANGELS

THE WAY OF THE SUN

WISDOM FROM WHITE EAGLE

Boxed sets of Affirmation Cards

FACE THE SUN

WINGS OF LIGHT

The Light Bringer

The Ray of John
and the Age of Intuition

WHITE EAGLE

THE WHITE EAGLE PUBLISHING TRUST
LISS · HAMPSHIRE · ENGLAND
www.whiteaglepublishing .org

THE LIGHTBRINGER first published May 2001
Reprinted May 2002

© The White Eagle Publishing Trust 2001

British Library Cataloguing in Publication Data

A Catalogue record for this book
is available from the British Library

ISBN 0-85487-116-0

Set in 12 on 15pt Arepo at the Publisher
and printed and bound in Great Britain at
the University Press, Cambridge

CONTENTS

INTRODUCTION:
A NEW MASTER FOR A NEW AGE

Now there was leaning on Jesus' bosom one of
his disciples, whom Jesus loved.

John 13 : 23

THE IDEA OF a new age beginning at around the present time in history is well-established, and arises from the astronomical position of the signs of the zodiac in relation to the earth and their apparent onward movement. Roughly every two thousand years, by what is known as the precession of the equinoxes, the earth comes under the influence of a new sign. At this time we are in the process of entering an age overshadowed by Aquarius and leaving that identified by Pisces. Coupled with this idea, in many minds, is the sense that just as the Piscean Age was ushered in by a great teacher, Jesus Christ, so an Aquarian Age teacher may also manifest.

White Eagle teaches that the new age does have a master, or world teacher, attached to it. He does not say that this teacher replaces Jesus Christ, and neither does he in any way devalue the other great teachers the world has seen, teachers such as Buddha and Mohammed. For him the term 'the Christ', the Son (or, equally the Daughter) of God, denotes a presence within all of us. It is the presence of the Christ in a teacher which makes him or her a great teacher, a world teacher. From this derives the great optimism of White Eagle's teaching: the sense that if we allow the Christ within to blossom and unfold, we too may reach masterhood; we too may reach a level at which we do not die, and leave the wheel of rebirth behind us. 'Every one of you,' he says, 'is your own saviour; and every one of you is the saviour of all humanity'.

He teaches that at the level at which they operate, beyond the wheel of rebirth, the separation of the Masters into personalities is not really necessary. The desire to identify personalities is a very 'earthly' one. However, he gives to the teacher for the new age the name 'John', linking this partly but perhaps subtly to the earthly personality of the 'disciple Jesus loved' (see the passage from St John's Gospel, quoted above).

When White Eagle began talking about the new world teacher and the Aquarian Age it was during the middle of the twentieth century, when the term 'the new age' was not the overloaded term it is today. In what he says, he makes no grand claims for himself, but his teaching (throughout which he claims only to be a spokesperson) does make claims for us all. Our birthright, whether we take up the challenge consciously or not, is a gradual unfolding of the spiritual senses, in accordance with spiritual law, until, by our own individual endeavours, we create for ourselves a golden age where heaven is established upon earth.

To some this may seem a romantic ideal, while others may look around and see the process of transformation already starting to take place in all kinds of attempts to see life on the planet as one whole and to respect it; and also in scientific exploration and discovery, in the ever more mystical approach to the basic substance of being that science offers, and in social projects that bring people together in brotherhood and equal opportunity.

White Eagle's loving words bring deep reassurance as well as insight. They may bring hope, too, to those who dread painful changes to the earth. What he has said about the future and the coming teacher spans a long period of his teaching, and great care has gone into bringing this together and making the line of thought as simple as possible.

Among those series of White Eagle's teachings which have been published is a complete commentary on St John's Gospel, under the title THE LIVING WORD OF ST JOHN. It forms a companion to the present volume.

The Preface to that book also gives some background to the circumstances in which the teachings were given, and describes a remarkable vision of St John which Grace Cooke, White Eagle's medium, received in the foothills of the Pyrenees in July 1931. It would be good to read THE LIVING WORD OF ST JOHN alongside the present book, for it helps to establish John as a teacher in his own right. His Gospel is very different from those of Matthew, Mark and Luke. According to scholarship, it shows an immersion in philosophies associated as much with the Greeks as with Jesus' own countrymen; according to tradition, it also shows at least some affinity with emerging ideas in Hinduism. Yet the words are ascribed to Jesus, and the reader must always ask what was John's special understanding, which enabled him to reproduce Jesus' words as he did.

We leave that question for the moment unanswered, for it is close to the subject of part of the book itself. What is White Eagle's own reason for confidence about who the new Master is; what is the basis for his own special understanding?

The name 'White Eagle' comes from the Native American tradition. There it implies a wise teacher. Among the attributes of the white eagle (which is not an actual species) is a unique ability to fly straight towards the sun. It is this unblinking flight towards the sun—the truth, God—that, to many of his readers, distinguishes White Eagle himself. In Christian symbolism, however, the eagle is the symbol of St John, just as that of St Mark is the lion, of St Luke the bull, and of St Matthew the man. In other words, through his name White Eagle associates himself by choice with St John, or at least with what he calls 'the ray of John'. He claims to be a spokesman for a group, rather than a teacher in his own right. He has said: 'White Eagle is—shall we suggest?—a sign, an influence, a ray, a group'. Thus the ray of John shines through this book, even if White Eagle would nowhere claim to be the teacher himself.

The White Eagle Lodge, founded according to White Eagle's instruction in 1936, was brought into being by the work 'behind the scenes' of illumined teachers whose symbol is the six-pointed Star. The name by which they are known in this book is 'the Star Brotherhood', which is not intended to be different from the old term 'the White Brotherhood', just less easily misunderstood. The central work of the White Eagle Lodge, mentioned from time to time in this book, is that of projecting the universal Christ healing light into the world, using the six-pointed Star as a focal point.

White Eagle says,

'All of you are Stars. Jesus, the great world teacher, came to earth under the pronouncement of the Star. It has taken the whole of the Piscean Age, which he ushered in, to bring human kind towards understanding of the meaning of the Star. Now as your feet are upon the path of the Aquarian Age, the Star is beginning to be known as the symbol of brotherhood, the symbol of the age of Aquarius, of which the Master Jesus spoke when he directed his disciples to follow the man with the water pot—the man who poured forth the water of the spirit upon the followers of the Star, all who are ready to receive.' Elsewhere he says, 'The Star of Bethlehem that we worship, salute and bow before ... is the keynote of human happiness'.*

This book seeks to show how the ray of John touches all our hearts, stimulating in us those qualities which will become more apparent as the age of the spirit advances. This ray helps us to bring heaven and earth closer together, on the earth itself and within ourselves, and to become more open to the spirit, emotionally, mentally, physically and psychologically—to learn how to work in greater harmony in groups and with the natural and angelic kingdoms. Through it, we also learn to develop the chakras and raise what White Eagle calls the solar fire, through a central focus on using the heart chakra in the service of all life. The ray of John thus seeks to be expressed in action and service. This is our future, and how soon or late we allow it to come depends on each of us.

*The quotations are from the White Eagle books THE WAY OF THE SUN (p. 92), and JESUS TEACHER AND HEALER (2000 edition, p. 117). There is a useful passage on the same subject in THE GENTLE BROTHER, chapter VI, section 6.

Some Definitions

The Christ

When White Eagle refers to 'the Christ' he means the universal spirit of love which dwells in each one of us, the part of us which is eternal and perfect. The Christ is also to be regarded as a disembodied being symbolised by the Sun—our link with the Great Spirit (whether you call Him–Her God, Allah, Jehovah) and as the 'Son' (actually Son–Daughter) of God within us, the Christ presence within makes us sons and daughters of God. White Eagle speaks of such a being as beyond gender: while 'Jesus' is the man of history, the man who most clearly embodied that Christ-spirit, there is no limitation to the male gender in either the person of God, the Christ or 'Golden One', or in the group known as 'the masters'.

St John

The St John referred to throughout (whether as 'the lightbringer', 'the 'lightbearer', 'the Beloved', 'the Divine', or 'St John the mystic') is of course the disciple of Jesus and writer of the Gospel, not John the Baptist. Elsewhere White Eagle refers to John as having manifested many times on earth. 'He is the forerunner, the great being who is so close to this new revelation of truth which humanity will receive at the appointed time of the Lord. You are working with the great pioneer, the lightbringer. He is in shining armour.'

Brotherhood

The term 'the brotherhood' is intended to have the same dual reference: 'brother–sisterhood' has been used in one chapterhead, but is too clumsy for the general flow. 'Brethren' is used in the book, and is not intended as a masculine term, but rather a non-gender-specific term for companions in spirit.

Master

The nature of 'a master' is defined in the book: here it may simply be said to be one who has achieved mastery over all the elements of life. White Eagle also speaks of angels and of guides; we hope they do not need defining except by stating that he regards each one of us as having a personal 'master' or 'teacher' and 'angelic guide'. When 'the Master' is meant to stand for the Christ, the word is capitalized.

The New Age

White Eagle writes of the Aquarian Age that is beginning, but he also writes of the golden age, the time when Christ comes in all his glory and we enter into the Golden City. Separate time-frames for the two have to be recognized, but his point appears to be that through our own creativity at the thought level we actually create a golden age, and there is no better time to concentrate on doing that than at the outset of a new astrological Age. The two are not entirely separable.

A Master for a New Age

Both this, and the question of how White Eagle actually regards St John, may best be addressed by comparison with the Buddhist idea of the boddhisatva. The boddhisatva is on a path to buddhahood, but vows not to leave the cycle of creation until all beings have attained enlightenment. There is thus a perpetual and onward development and creation of souls at the highest level, and we individually have the opportunity to move to this level, with the same vow of service animating our actions. In this book, White Eagle actually ends with the principle of service to all life. His teaching is not identical to the Buddhist one, but the boddhisatva idea may be helpful in understanding White Eagle's concepts.

Biblical and Other Quotations

The bible is quoted from the Authorized Version of 1611. This is the version White Eagle normally quoted from in the talks that make up the book, because of its familiarity to his listeners. Any quotations that are regarded as important references are given in the headnote to the chapter, and all biblical quotations (and related quotations, such as those from the liturgy) are represented by italics.

The headnotes are intended to be like epigraphs: that is, they contain seed thoughts for the chapter and are not simply references for later quotations. They should therefore be read as part of the text.

I

THE TEACHERS
AND THEIR WORK

Now there was leaning on Jesus' bosom one of his disciples, whom Jesus loved.

John 13 : 23

And ye shall know the truth, and the truth shall make you free.

John 8 : 32

If ye love me, keep my commandments. And I will pray the Father, and he shall give you another Comforter, that he may abide with you for ever; even the Spirit of truth; whom the world cannot receive, because it seeth him not, neither knoweth him: but ye know him; for he dwelleth with you, and shall be in you.
I will not leave you comfortless: I will come to you.

John 14 : 15–18

Again, a new commandment I write unto you, which thing is true in him and in you: because the darkness is past, and the true light now shineth.
He that saith he is in the light, and hateth his brother, is in darkness even until now.

He that loveth his brother abideth in the light, and there is none occasion of stumbling in him.

But he that hateth his brother is in darkness, and walketh in darkness, and knoweth not whither he goeth, because that darkness hath blinded his eyes.

1 John 2 : 8–11

And I saw a new heaven and a new earth: for the first heaven and the first earth were passed away; and there was no more sea.

And I John saw the holy city, new Jerusalem, coming down from God out of heaven, prepared as a bride adorned for her husband.

Revelation 21 : 1–2

WE COME TO you under the name of White Eagle, but would explain that we speak for a large company of shining beings, angels and illumined souls of men and women who are sometimes referred to as the Star Brotherhood.

We have the name of White Eagle because our message is the message of John, the beloved of the Lord Jesus. John is the lightbringer; White Eagle is a humble servant, but the symbol of the white eagle is one used by John the Beloved, the teacher of the new age of Aquarius. This light is gradually being born upon your earth plane. Many messengers are coming to the earth from the higher spheres of life with the same message.

It is a very simple message, the one which Jesus left with his disciples—*love one another.*

We have worked for many incarnations in the personality we take on when we come into physical conditions, to bring to men and women an understanding of the brotherhood of all life, so that the kingdom of God shall come upon earth. But this can only happen when you have discovered that within your own souls is the light of the spirit of Christ, the Christ light which is the seed given to every one of you. Let us talk further about this light.

Jesus spoke of the Comforter; he said that the Comforter would come; that by the Comforter you would know truth, and the truth would set you free. We tell you that the Comforter is this inner light which we call love; it is the love which Christ, the supreme Light of all human kind, brought to the earth. You have been given the power to see for yourself this Christ light working in the heart of your brother and your sister. Seek for the gentle love of the lord Christ in your brothers and sisters, and if you cannot see it immediately, nonetheless by your own efforts to love them you will in time evoke in them a response. This is the law of brotherhood: to look for love, to give love in all your ways; to live purely and kindly, to treat Mother Earth with consideration and thoughtfulness, to respect all life and not to shed the blood of any creature; to give love and to help life to a higher and more beautiful form on the earth.

This is the first part of our message. The second is again the one which John the Beloved received and recorded in the book of Revelation when he spoke of 'a new heaven and a new earth'. If you will study that vision, you will come to realize that the new heaven is in you yourself, and that you have within your soul the power to rise up into those higher realms of life and light, and enter into the glories of that heaven world in full consciousness.

A world teacher is one through whom the light shines without being obscured. Now you want to know if there is to be another world teacher for the Aquarian Age. You realize, of course, that there is always the one supreme Son of life? In Christianity this being is called Jesus Christ. The name of the next world teacher might possibly be John Christ. What we are trying to show you is that the great Light can shine through any human vehicle. Through other world teachers the same Light will someday shine, but on a higher spiral of life. It is not the person, but his or her radiation through the ages that makes him or her a world teacher.

Do not therefore think of the world teacher merely as an individual. While the light and the glory will manifest through the personality, it will not be limited by that personality, but will be working like the leaven in the bread to stimulate the individual life to higher levels, to raise the vibrations of the earth itself. You see, the world teacher does not come alone; such a being brings his or her disciples. Many are working at the present time to make ready for the new world teacher, and are already being used by their master to raise the vibrations. Some of you may even be numbered with these disciples.

How will the new world teacher come? As a personality, yes, but since the new age of Aquarius is going to bring forth the occult powers in you all—is going to tear down the veil of the temple, so that you can see into the spiritual realms, into the higher life—it necessarily follows that the teacher will come from the higher world. Such teachers will not necessarily enter the body of a newborn babe, but bodies prepared for that great soul. Yes, much as the body of Jesus was prepared for many years until the master Jesus was able to give it to the great world teacher who is worshipped and loved as the Christ. Yes, we may tell you that in the new age there will come a great illumination from the spiritual realms upon the people of earth. There will be one particular teacher, it is true, but there will also be many disciples who will work with him or her from the world of spirit. Already the streams of light are preparing human kind to recognize the new world teacher, who will bring the same, old message.

The second coming is stimulating the soul qualities in men and women. You may call them psychic qualities—if you like, psychic powers—because they refer to the psyche or the soul, which is the next body, the finer body. In the future the physical body, which is of a lower vibration, will gradually change and become as the soul body is, as the psychic body. As men and women open their inner eyes to the world of light, so the whole vibration, the whole physical substance of the body will change and become pure, and will become as a master's body.

Individuals react to this great spiritual light in different ways, and they do not understand why. They feel a tremendous urge, a pushing forward, a desire to assert themselves, a desire to introduce brotherhood in the crudest form. Behind all such crudeness is the impetus, the power of the great Light of the world teacher.

Only when the spirit within is awakened, when your eyes are opened to the heavens, do you behold the coming of the Master in the silence of your innermost being. The second coming will not so much be an outward, but an inner manifestation. You are looking forward to the second coming of Christ, for it is said so clearly that Christ would come again; but we have said on many occasions that this second coming will be in the heart of every man and woman. It will be the awakening of the light.

We want you to understand that spirituality is not something quiescent, but strong and powerful, finer than the matter of earth, finer than the vibration of earth. It is the substance of its life. So it is true that as a man or woman becomes sensitive to the love of God, as he or she desires to become Christlike, so he or she brings through into physical life this power, this spiritual force. As the person goes about his or her business, other people feel this force in exactly the same way as you see a light which is switched on in a room. The person who has the inner light takes that light wherever he or she goes. Thus it is that the vibration or name of Christ which sounds throughout the earth (for the vibration *is* the name) is the vibration of light and is felt and seen. Many people recognize that there are those who seem to bring healing or a light as they enter a room, although they do not understand the nature of this. Those who recognize the light instantly acknowledge it. They bow in their souls, in their minds; in this way they bend the knee to the vibration of Christ, the Son.

All through his ministry the disciple most closely associated with Jesus was John—John the Beloved, whom he called to sit by his side during the Last Supper. It is significant that John was by the side of Jesus when all the disciples partook of the Last Supper before the master was crucified; and that in his last words on the cross Jesus commended John to his mother Mary.

In the new age of Aquarius into which humanity is slowly moving, there is a unification or a drawing together of the two—the master Jesus and the great and beloved St John. Read carefully the Gospel of St John and the Revelation of St John, and you will find in all those teachings reference to the inner powers of every human being, and symbolism referring to each man and woman's own soul and its potentialities.

You will remember also that before the Last Supper Jesus gave instructions to his chosen disciples to go before him into the town to find the inn where there was an upper room; the disciples were to follow the man carrying the water pot. This was the symbol of the new age of Aquarius which was to follow the Piscean Age, in which Jesus came to give his particular message to human kind, a simple message of love. Yet, if you study the teachings of Jesus of Nazareth with knowledge, you will realize the profundity as well as the simplicity of his teaching.

Jesus came to teach the people how to live the life on the physical plane within their communities. But John began to teach people the purpose of Jesus' teaching, because it is only when men and women can live the life of love and brotherhood towards each other that they can then begin to develop those soul powers of which we speak, those heavenly powers with which God the heavenly Father–Mother has endowed them. The new age then is of John—the age of Brotherhood! The Aquarian Age is the age of St John the Mystic.

We are moving onwards, upwards, until we reach the zenith of the great circle, where shines the Throne of God ... from which emanated the message of John.

II

THE MESSAGE OF JOHN

In the beginning was the Word, and the Word was with God, and the Word was God.

The same was in the beginning with God. All things were made by Him; and without Him was not any thing made that was made. In Him was life; and the life was the light of men.

John 1 : 1–4

Now there stood by the cross of Jesus his mother, and his mother's sister, Mary the wife of Cleophas, and Mary Magdalene.

When Jesus therefore saw his mother, and the disciple standing by, whom he loved, he saith unto his mother, Woman, behold thy son! Then saith he to the disciple, Behold thy mother! And from that hour that disciple took her unto his own home.

John 19 : 25–27

The first day of the week cometh Mary Magdalene early, when it was yet dark, unto the sepulchre.... Jesus saith unto her, Mary. She turned herself, and saith unto him, Rabboni; which is to say, Master.

John 20 : 1, 16

ONLY WITH the dawning of a new age will men and women begin to comprehend the mystery contained in the opening phrases of John's Gospel. The message of John has never been to the human mind. John spoke to the soul of the world. The teachings of the beloved John contain the mystery of the human soul; those of Jesus refer primarily to the divine Light of the spirit within the soul. These same teachings were given in other forms in the ancient wisdom, but never as these ... never so simply, so profoundly.

St John the Divine is an ancient and great Spirit, or source of wisdom. The human vehicle or manifestation known generally as St John was brought into being by the descent of one of the great Beings about the throne of God. This is a statement most difficult for you to comprehend; neither can the finite mind appreciate the worth, magnitude, truth and beauty of this teaching and its revelation. The revelation (in this we include all the writings attributed to John) came from a high source, or plane of spiritual power.

The Gospel of St John sets out a code of conduct which the initiated cannot help but follow. It is not a question of 'You must be good. You must love your brother or sister'. Rather it is that when illumination comes there is only one way in which it is possible to live, and that is by spontaneous love, kindness, gentleness, not only to brother man, or to the sister of your spirit, but to all creation.

An earnest study of the message of John reveals that he taught concerning the power of the soul.* His coming heralded the Aquarian Age, the age when human beings will arise in spiritual light; when men and women will learn to use the full power of the soul. They will do this by reason of knowledge concerning each and all of the vehicles comprising that temple which is man–woman. The divine Revelation of St John contains an outline of universal evolution from the beginning to the end. St John is he who is yet to come—yes, in fuller manifestation—to the children of earth. He came then in lesser degree with his 'beloved', known to people there as Jesus of Nazareth, to help him in his work;

*For a clear exposition of this, see White Eagle's book THE LIVING WORD OF ST JOHN (White Eagle Publishing Trust, second edition, 2000)

but will return, this time in all his glory. These two brought to this earth planet the divine message of the Christ love.

The Mystical Marriage

When we use the name 'John', do not limit it to the one personality of which you are cognizant. Remember there is a great being who is the leader of the Aquarian Age.... The Master, the world teacher, at the head of the Aquarian Age is the John man. We do not say the St John of your bible; we say John, the Man of God, the man who is glorified in the Father–Mother. Remember that every soul has two aspects, and you may call these masculine and feminine, male and female, and the masters have manifested and do manifest at times in one or other aspect of their twin being, their twin soul. This is a profound mystery. But the one who is the head of the Aquarian Age, who comes in full glory into the world through man, is known as John, the Divine John. And the church or religion of this new age of Aquarius will be the religion of brotherhood, when old forms will be swept away. There will be neither church nor state as you know it at present. Do not be fearful of our words, because then there comes the glorious birth to bring golden light, ushering in the golden age.

The lapse of two thousand years therefore reveals not one but two souls of great purity and beauty, who brought to the world the Light of the ages. It reveals a close and deep affinity between the two: so close. What then was John to the Master?

To the careful onlooker it would appear that John was necessary to the work of the Master, since John was ever one of the three called upon when the Master exercised the divine power in any unusual degree. Was it not John, as we have said, who was seated beside Jesus in that upper room prepared for the holy communion of the spirit? Moreover, is it not said that he actually laid his head upon the Master's breast? And out of all His followers and disciples, at the crucifixion, did not the dying Jesus give His mother into the care of John? What can be the interpretation of this supreme commission and trust? And why was John called 'the beloved' of the Master?

These two, Jesus and John, show forth the Mystical Marriage. Do not obscure such a glorious truth as this by your grosser conceptions of the subject of sex. Nothing can be further from reality. But in the mystical marriage between soul and spirit will be seen, indeed, the perfect—perfected—union which all humanity may hope, aeons hence, to know and experience.

Jesus, a spirit, an individual being, came forth from the bright and morning star: Jesus, who personifies to most of us that innermost part of the heart of each man and woman in which God abides—and John too, who might embody (if you really understood) that soul of humanity which craves and loves the light. Did those two come to earth already knowing, yet for a time foregoing, the purity and the wonder of that complete union of heart, emotion and thought?

A close relationship exists between the planet Venus and this earth. Some may question this; science doubts the possibility of life existing on any other planet. Well, you see upon this altar behind me as I speak a six-pointed Star, the symbol of a Brotherhood.* As surely as you see the Star, we know that we have witnessed the dawn break upon the planet Venus; and we know that you, that every human soul, will migrate in time to beyond this darker globe to that bright and morning Star. Venus—the planet of harmony, beauty, love—is where souls, passed beyond earthly influence and stress, dwell in completion—dual souls, in that sublime condition of perfected marriage!

Have you not also dreamt of a human love made perfect, of two souls blended as one in perfect love? There such dreams find rich fulfilment; souls find themselves, each in the other. At will, each soul may withdraw and go its separate way; at will, they merge one into the other. For dual souls, or affinities, are both aspects of the one being, perfected: of man–woman as conceived by the Father–Mother and held in His–Her mind always.

John is so close to Jesus, so close that the two are all but inseparable,

*The talk on which this paragraph was based was given in the White Eagle Lodge in London, where a three-dimensional six-pointed Star in glass crystal hangs over the altar. This is the basis for the illustration used in this book at the chapter head.

two aspects of the one truth. And following the great world teacher whom you know as Jesus of Nazareth, comes the other aspect of that one, the aspect which we understand as the Light, the divine Light: John the Lightbearer, John who is so close to the Divine Mother because of what Jesus said at his crucifixion: *Behold thy Mother.*

The coming of the age of Aquarius will certainly bring into prominence the Mother, or the woman aspect of life. In other words, it is indicative of the development of intuition, or increase of soul power among the people of the earth. The First Principle, being representative of the Father, or the Will, must be balanced by the Mother, or the Intuition. When you get perfect interplay of these two Principles—the first of Will or Power, and the other of Love and Wisdom—then is brought forth the Christ child.*

Do not mistake our meaning. The human self contains both manly and womanly qualities. In the male, the first predominate; in the female, the second. Each individual soul passes through many trials, tribulations and initiations. By this process these two Principles of Will and Love gradually become united and perfectly balanced, with the result that the Christ child is eventually born within. This is the true meaning of the immaculate conception, which is the outcome of the mystical marriage between spirit and soul within each man and woman. The immaculate conception is the perfect blending of the intuition and the spiritual qualities of the mother, together with that mind which is representative of divine will and energy: the divine will and energy impregnates the divine love and wisdom. When you get this perfect blending, this perfect marriage within your innermost being, there is the production of a perfect son–daughter of God within you. We would draw your attention to the symbol of the six-pointed Star, which consists of two interwoven triangles and is an emblem of this mystical marriage—the perfect blending of the dual aspects of life.

Let us bring this right down to the physical plane. What do we see in the world today? Why is there such terrible suffering? Because humanity has starved itself of the Mother principle for many centuries.

*White Eagle is hinting at the three principles, or persons, of the Trinity.

There has been domination, first by the body and then by the intellect or brain. Both have tended to imprison, if not slay, the divine Mother principle, which is wisdom and love. In the future there will come this illumination, this initiation, this expansion of spiritual consciousness. You will see this mother aspect—not merely woman, for we are speaking of divine principles—you will see this divine principle of the Mother slowly but surely influencing the world. As a result, there will be a much greater inflow of love and wisdom; a lessening of the power-complex which, working through the human brain, causes individuals to produce the most diabolical machinery for the destruction of life. When the spirit of the Mother works hand in hand with the true Father principle (which is the higher, the divine mind), you will get a return to sanity, to harmony, to happiness.

As the years go by you will see women less and less excluded from high office, but given their correct, honourable places in the affairs of the world. The soul, or the woman aspect of your make-up, is that aspect which inspires praise and worship. It is the soul that is stirred in religious service. Music can arouse the soul. The ritual of religion can stimulate and stir the soul. And all the time the soul is developing this feeling, this intuition, which is enabling the spirit to contact matter, to come into greater manifestation in matter.

The woman aspect, the divine Mother aspect, is the tenderness, the love and the gentleness in life without which spiritual death must ensue. As we have said, when the people of earth can return to the worship of the beautiful Mother, the source of all life, there will be a return to happiness. On the day of Jesus' resurrection it is significant that the first person to arrive at the tomb was a woman; for the other disciples might not like a woman being the first to carry the glad tidings. In the new age of Aquarius it is the woman aspect of life—not necessarily women but the mother aspect of the spirit of life—which will always recognize the master. In other words, this means that it is the loving, tender, gentle and feminine attributes in either men or women which will first behold the Lord Christ.

III

THE GREAT EARTH-CYCLES

*And God said, Let there be light: and there was light. And God saw
the light, that it was good: and God divided the light from the darkness.*
Genesis 1 : 3–4

A GREAT CYCLE takes about twenty-five thousand years, and in that
cycle there are twelve ages. These being divided out equally come to
slightly over two thousand years each. We are not being too precise
about the number of years. During each age the earth planet comes
under a certain zodiacal influence, and this influence affects the
thoughts, the spiritual development and also your material life, and in
particular your spiritual and religious life.

Many different ways of developing this soul-consciousness within
have been taught throughout time by the Sages, and in accordance with
the zodiacal sign then prevailing; because each age brings to the earth a
special and separate planetary and angelic influence. Human nature as
a whole, containing within it the influences of all the twelve zodiacal
signs, responds—but according to the rung of the ladder, or cycle on
the spiral of life, on which the individual soul happens to be.

Going back in time we see that it is the Taurean influence which
runs through ancient Egyptian religions. Next, in immediately pre-Chris-
tian times, it was the sign of Aries—the Ram—which was the ruling

influence. In this Arietian Age, worship of the Lamb is to be found in Jewish religious rites; while during the Piscean Age—the age of the Fish—we find the descent of spirit into deepest matter.

The great teacher of the Piscean Age, Jesus, the Christ, was a great mystic, a great psychic, a great healer; and in his life can be traced his response to the higher influences of the Piscean Age—that is, to the Neptunian influence. Not many can respond to the influence of Neptune sufficiently to bring through into activity the Neptunian ray. In Jesus, however, we see a wonderful example of the perfect human being, who is responding in his physical life to the highest planetary influence of his age, and is thus an example of the preparation for the next stage in the great cycle, the age of Aquarius. He had responded to the angelic forces at their very apex. He was a true psychic, in the highest sense, because his psyche, or soul, was perfected and poised: a perfect channel; a calm and beautiful sea upon which the light of the sun was reflected clearly and beautifully. He walked upon the sea—a demonstration, not of his miraculous powers over nature, but to teach those of his disciples with understanding that he was able to control the soul, the emotions. He had risen above the turbulence of the desire-vehicles of life. He was responding steadily, steadfastly, to that higher octave of his physical life ... to his ruler, Neptune.

In sleep, the soul which is made ready will respond to the gentle influence of Neptune, and will enjoy experiences on the higher planes. If the physical body is sufficiently attuned and has been purified through right thinking and positive life, then the mind or memory will catch a memory of these experiences. Then the Piscean influence will illumine the soul and prepare it for the next step, which is the age of Aquarius.

We are now moving into that truly glorious period of the earth's evolution, the commencement of the new age; and Saturn—which on the lower vibration will bring tears and suffering and restrictions and limitation—has a wonderful influence upon the Aquarian being. We would say that Saturn is the portal of initiation; that as the soul draws near to release from bondage (I do not mean death, but release from what you call sin and desire), then the Saturnian influence will teach the soul how to hear the Word. This mysterious Word will enable the soul to pass through the portals of initiation into the mysteries of its own being, of its creation, evolution and final illumination and birth into the light of the Sun.

Furthermore, those sufficiently advanced on the spiral to respond to the higher octave, Uranus, find that suddenly there breaks upon their consciousness understanding ... light. Through the Uranian influence come sudden happenings: cataclysmic, revolutionary, turning night into day. Here we witness the sword of the Archangel Michael, as it descends upon men and women to release them, through suffering, to their glorious birth into the new and radiant life.

You must translate these truths onto the physical, the soul, and the spiritual planes of being. Let us recognize that when something cruel and devastating comes and sweeps away all that the human self holds and cherishes, and destroys the ideal for which it has worked and striven, then this is the sword of the great Archangel at work. Next comes resentment—but all too hastily. For even as the soul cries out in rebellion against God and all the angels in heaven, the light breaks through the mists, and there comes the calm and beauty of the morning sunlight, after the night of stress and storm. And in your thankfulness you forget the storm, and know only joy at your rebirth and the hour of peace.

The individual thinks he or she is very powerful; nations think they are powerful; but all are as nothing against the mighty law of the cosmos. The hand of God, working through natural forces, works in tune with the great planetary influences which will bring into operation on your earth plane the law of brotherhood. You cannot upset cosmic law. A few poor little nations cannot upset cosmic law.

The world is under the influence of Saturn at the present time, and in the same way that old Saturn is the guide which leads the individual to the altar of initiation, so Saturn will lead the nations too to the altar of initiation—initiation into the great brotherhoods. Saturn is doing its work right well!

Uranus that great—we might say 'benefic'—planet may be a little startling in its actions, and its influence may cause you to jump a little bit! But have no fear. All things are working together for good, and the man or woman who loves God must see it. When things happen, do not say in a foolish way, 'How terrible!'. Leave God to know God's work, and God's great angels to know their work, for they are always working to put right the foolish mistakes of human kind. Wonderful happenings will in fact be taking place which are bringing to human kind the age of progress and of brotherhood, the age of liberation and of culture, the greater understanding of God's love and power. God, through the agency of the planets and the planetary beings, is shaking human kind up a little, but gradually the true and glorious spirit of brotherhood will take the place of outworn politics. The vision of John embraces the whole, from alpha to omega.

A Greater View

Human kind is now preparing for the great spiritual reconstruction which is to come. We endeavour to bring you somewhat of the light which has come to us. We do not say you must believe these things, but only reveal that which we have found in the temples of wisdom. May you find these words give you encouragement. If you feel your world is in a state of chaos, do not think of the so-called 'chaos', or share in thoughts of darkness, fear and doubt. You may be sorely tempted to go with the tide and to expect the worst; but we ask you, as children of the new age, to make it almost a ritual in your life not to participate in thoughts or words of doubt, fear or negation. Be positive, be constructive, for the wise child of the living God is able to penetrate the mists and darkness with a ray of light direct from the heart of God.

Always remember that the vibrations which emanate direct from the God-centre will penetrate through the mists of the densest matter. You who wish to participate in this great work of spiritual reconstruction must resolutely obey the highest command within you. You must love the Lord your God *with all your heart, with all your soul and with all your mind.* With heart, with emotion, with your whole mental body, you must love the Lord your God, and see in the darkness and chaos the seed of light, of God, which is there germinating. You can enter into the deepest depths of hell and there find God.

In the process of becoming God-conscious, the soul has clothed itself in many garments. It has passed through a process of involution, clothing itself, creating the subtler bodies. In each of the long stages of its being, it has acquired a subtler body. Think of these garments as being placed upon it through every age. We are not dealing with time as you understand it, but rather with a vastness—eternity. However, it is not until the individual is released from the finite mind that he or she can understand eternity. Eternity is now. It has always been and always will be. *As it was in the beginning is now and ever shall be, world without end.* Can you, through endeavouring to glimpse eternity, get a real understanding of those great cycles of life, or the ages of which we have spoken? One intermingling with the other, one breaking from another, one being born from another, even as the planets are born from the sun, and the systems of the universe are born from each other and from the whole. It is stupendous!

As the individual spark comes from the heart of God, without consciousness of its true nature, so becoming man–woman it creates those subtle bodies which it is now using by the process of its experience. We have reached the outermost rung of human evolution in the density of this earth plane. With the creation of the developed intellect which man–woman has now acquired, it would appear that humanity has reached the limit of involution. Now humanity turns its face upward. It has bottomed the depths, and now faces the upward arc; it reaches towards the angelic life.

The Aquarian Age, we would say, is the age wherein humanity becomes conscious of its real nature. Look about you, those who feel you have attained some knowledge, and see your brethren! Sometimes you may find yourself asking if they have a spirit at all? They may seem to be so full of the animal desires and passions, so far removed from the angelic state. You witness with saddened heart the clamouring for blood, the desire to fight and put down the other man or woman, the struggling for supremacy. But do not be harsh. As you see struggle and passion and lust take possession of these your brethren, try to understand what it is that grows within; see a seed struggling for expression. In the Aquarian Age, there will descend to the earth a tremendous outpouring from the Sun, such a vibration, such energy, such light as you cannot at present comprehend.

At the time of the crucifixion of the body of the Master Jesus, there was released a vital spirit. It was a world baptism. It has taken long, according to your understanding, for this vital body of the Son to permeate the particles or atoms of the human body. For all have been part of that baptism. Within your body flows a lifegiving stream from the vital body of the Christ.

Have you ever thought that the crucifixion is in fact a crucifixion which is still continually taking place with every violation and denial of the Christ-being which is living in the heart of every member of the human race? When you consider thus, you become sensitive, do you not, and think it terrible? But we say to you, do not think so. We would rather create the impression of a glorious and continual growth taking place in human kind. When you suffer grievous pain and come up against harsh conditions, you are crucified. But will it help you if White Eagle tells you that when you are crucified you are very close to the great awakening, to the resurrection, when you will find greater beauty, and more satisfying, deeper happiness, than you have ever known before? So, when crucifixion comes into your life, whatever form it takes, remember that after crucifixion follows the resurrection, and after the resurrection follows the ascension.

IV

THE FUTURE—THE AGE
OF BROTHERHOOD

Come, see a man, which told me all the things that ever I did.

John 4 : 29

Eye hath not seen, nor ear heard ... the glories which God hath prepared for them that love him.

1 Corinthians 2 : 9

Your young men shall see visions, and your old men shall dream dreams.

Acts 2 : 17

WE SHOULD LIKE to speak with you about your future. We do not often talk about your future, and indeed you have been taught that it is unwise to probe into it. Nevertheless, there is only one way in which a soul can learn to read its own future, and that is by understanding its past. You have always existed, because you are a seed of the infinite eternal Spirit; and when you understand the governing laws of life—and that every action, every word and every thought is impressed upon finer ethers, an impression which is there for all time—then you will realize how it is that the future can be foretold.

At a certain stage in human development a man or woman learns how to enter the eternal silence and read these records. Through them he or she learns that actions, words and thoughts, like seeds sown in the ground, unfailingly produce an effect. What that effect or outcome is, is no less than the future of the man or woman's soul. This is the true way of reading the future, for life is governed by a divine law which states that as the soul sows, it will surely reap.* Your future, then, is stored in the present. As you think, speak and act today, so you are sowing the seeds for tomorrow's harvest.

This is how the Masters of the Wisdom are able to read the future, both of the individual and of the human race. They are able to see quite clearly your soul's future. You will remember how the Master Jesus astounded the woman at the well by quietly telling her all about her past life. In the same way, he knew her future; and she went away and said: *'Come, see a man, which told me all the things that ever I did!'*.†

You have it in your power, when you have learnt to control your senses and emotions, to rise above the limited consciousness of your physical life and go through into those higher planes; to enter into the finer ethers which interpenetrate gross physical matter, and see the glory of God's plan of creation, which is beyond the capacity of the finite mind to understand. As you unfold spiritually, the limitations fall away; and you can enter into the finer ethers of the heavenly realms and there see God's plan for your future and for the future of all souls.

You have been told there is to be a second coming of Christ, the Lord of this earth planet. When is this to be? There is ample evidence that the time draws near, and this is shown particularly in the soul-preparation of many whom you encounter. You witness rapid growth of spiritual qualities in humanity; you contact the vibrations of the Christ body in the new religions of your day. You are being taught the way of life for this advancing time, both by purity of thought and aspiration, and by purification of the physical vehicle—why, it has become an instinct in many of you to eat pure food, to claim the perfect health

*Galatians 6 : 7
†The whole story is told in chapter 4 of St John's Gospel

and harmony which is your birthright! There is aspiration in you. The Christ above and the Christ within alike are raising you to meet Him–Her on that higher plane of consciousness, when the Christ comes in all power and glory.

Will Christ eventually come again in a physical body? Christ will manifest to the men and women of earth in a vehicle like their own, only of a very pure and fine vibration. Preparations are going forward, and before the Christ comes in all glory there will already be established on earth a universal brotherhood of the spirit. And you will see initiates, masters, permanently established on earth; you will see them directing and controlling the affairs of the world. With this coming there will be a manifestation of many of the masters, those illumined souls who belong to the ancient and secret brotherhood at work 'within the veil' (we mean on the other side of life) for the emancipation and enlightenment of humanity. These will come forth and mingle with humanity, and many will recognize them; but those who recognize a master must already have a degree of mastership themselves.

You will see great changes upon earth at the dawn of the new age. When Christ came, two thousand years ago, it was to rend the veil and to open the way to all to tread the path of initiation. Humanity has since been prepared and educated along a certain path, and now we tread the higher spiral, ready to receive the full outpouring, and the raising up through the spirit of Christ, the beloved Son.

The Way to the Age of the Spirit

It is not only a few selected ones who attain mastership or Christhood. All the children of God have their feet set upon the selfsame path. But there are qualifications required of the soul. It must first of all recognize that life is a vast brotherhood. This sounds so simple and easy. All of us long for brotherhood; that is, we all want other people to be brotherly towards us, but we do not always find it easy to feel brotherly towards other people, and other forms of life—except towards people and things we find it easy to like, or towards our pet animals. It is not easy to feel brotherly towards animals when we still desire to eat their flesh. Yet to eat that flesh is bound to retard the evolution of our soul, because it creates disharmony in the physical atoms, and is against the law of brotherhood.

The Aquarian Age will see a great development and unfoldment of the human soul and spirit. The soul as well as the spirit is like a seed, or like a babe. It has to develop and unfold all the qualities of the parent. Do you see what we mean? You are children, having within you potential mastership and Christhood. You have been given freewill and the exact conditions which you most need for the unfoldment of your character, soul and spirit. A seed or bulb contains all the beauties of the flower, and you say: 'What a miracle! Out of that tiny seed has come this glorious flower!'. Is that not an illustration of every human life, growing from the soul seed and the spirit seed? The spirit, the seed-atom, sown in the heart chakra, is the seed of the Christ. You confront the conditions most necessary during your incarnations to develop that seed and bring forth a perfected soul, and a flowering of the Christ spirit.

If you could keep to this one viewpoint, it would help you so much in your daily life, giving you patience and courage to persevere with the wonderful piece of work that has been entrusted to you. No matter who or what you are, it is your work. As humanity develops, physical discoveries will make life easier and better; men and women will also develop soul powers which will enable them to penetrate worlds of finer ethers. In your meditations you are just on the fringe of this form of psychic development. To all of you we would say, 'This is the way'; for only through deeper and deeper meditation will you reach a clearer understanding and picture of the future, and of the path which you are travelling. You will arrive at a more profound happiness as you grow to understand what you are doing, and where you are going.

Presently, you will be faced with one unshakeable truth. You will come to a barrier across which you cannot move until you have completely mastered the lesson of brotherhood. You have to recognize and realize this, and become one with all life, through love. Until you can do this you remain at a standstill. No more curtains or veils will be withdrawn for you until that barrier has been safely crossed.

In the process of development, men and women discard the veils which shield them from this vast array of spiritual power. *Eye hath not seen, nor ear heard ... the glories which God hath prepared for them that love him*—that is, for those men and women who reach heaven. This is your future and this is worth striving for. When you are distracted by material things, keep very calm, keep very still. Remember the Brethren of the Silence, whose very power of achievement lies in silence. Touch the silence, and the power of the spirit will flow into you and disperse all your fears.

We have said many, many times: 'Nothing is so important as God'. There are many very clever people with great intellectual development, but despite all their knowledge, they are unable to penetrate the higher ethers or touch this profound spiritual silence; and indeed, until you have developed the required spiritual qualities, you will never penetrate these finer ethers.

The age of Aquarius is the age of spirit, the age when, as your bible says, there will be a great outpouring of the divine Spirit upon the young and the old. *Your young men shall see visions, and your old men shall dream dreams.* As you know, the symbol of Aquarius is the man carrying the water pot, pouring forth the waters of life. Life cannot continue on the earth without water; and as the precession of the equinoxes continues, there comes a time and age when the waters of heaven, the waters of the spirit, are poured forth to stimulate the spiritual growth of humanity.

Without this growth of the human soul and spirit there would come devastation. Yet God is omnipotent, all-power; God is omniscient, all-wise (the all-wise Mother aspect); and God is omnipresent, ever-present. God is in everyone, in every creature, in all nature. God is in the air you breathe. God is in every cell of your body. God is closer than breathing, nearer than hands and feet, because God and you are one—but you do not know it yet. You have not burst the bonds of the physical consciousness and do not realize that you are potentially yourself a God.

In the silence you will find your Creator; and through this you will penetrate those higher worlds. Your eyes will be opened to the glories that exist there and death will no longer have any power over you.

It is true, there is no death. When you have passed the great barrier, you will be amazed and say: 'But I did not feel anything! Am I dead? I feel exactly the same'. There is no difference, except you have taken off one dress and left it behind. You are no longer interested in it. That is all that death means. You are eternal and as you are today, so you will be tomorrow. As you create yourself, and build the spiritual atoms into your soul, you will be able to enjoy the fruits which the Lord has prepared for you in the higher state of life.

If you find it difficult to restrain and control yourself when you want to, at those moments take a deep breath and say to yourself many times: 'God is with me'. Then be still and let All Good manifest through you. You do not know how much benefit will come from this practice.

Can you feel the angelic presences as you read our words? Cannot you feel their love and the purity of their souls? They draw so close to you. With them we say to you: 'Forward, forward, forward, my children, gaining every day in spiritual qualities and powers which will be the most holy and blessed part of your life and the lives of all men and women in the future'.

V

THE AQUARIAN AGE

These are they which came out of great tribulation, and have washed their robes, and made them white in the blood of the Lamb.

Revelation 7: 14

I was in the spirit on the Lord's day, and heard behind me a great voice, as of a trumpet.

Revelation 1 : 10

Behold: I shew you a mystery; We shall not all sleep, but we shall be changed,

In a moment, in the twinkling of an eye, at the last trump: for the trumpet shall sound, and the dead shall be raised incorruptible, and we shall be changed.

For this corruptible must put on incorruption, and this mortal must put on immortality.

1 Corinthians 15 : 51–53

For now we see through a glass, darkly; but then face to face: now I know in part; but then shall I know even as I am known.

1 Corinthians 13 : 12

YOU STAND at the gateway of a new age, and many of you are wondering what this age will bring to human kind. The answer largely depends upon how far men and women are prepared to rise above materialism and accept the truth of a spiritual life, the fact that they are spiritual beings. Beyond your physical body and the personality known to your companions on earth is your true self, which has descended from the spheres of light—your true home—to manifest on earth. It is impossible yet for that self to manifest fully through the lower vehicles, because they are not ready to receive that beautiful spirit; but you are preparing these vehicles, the emotional, mental, etheric and all the finer bodies, in your daily life. When through discipline and initiation your lower vehicles are ready, then your spirit will be able to manifest, to a great degree, through your physical form.

A new age is like a new year. For many people it is usual to make resolutions at the beginning of the year. On the other hand an equal number of people refrain, saying that resolutions are only made to be broken. We suggest that good resolutions are steps on the upward pathway; every effort which the soul makes to rise above an inferior to a superior state will benefit the character. No such effort is ever lost, but is a step on the path of light which will lead you all eventually to the state which is known as the golden age.

Many people ask, 'How can we know that we even approach such an age? Can it be possible?'. We know, my brethren, because we have studied the records of the past, which tell us that humanity has lived in such golden ages before. One of your great scientists* refers to certain evolved and advanced souls which he regards as representing the peaks of humanity. If there are peaks of human achievement spiritually as well as materially, there must be an apex at which humanity collectively arrives during the process of life. We speak of what we have found in the akashic records. Human kind has lived before in a state of perfection, harmony, beauty and love. Then came the inevitable decline; and now again the upward climb.

Let us tell you of a man who became satiated with material life. He had achieved all he had attempted; he possessed all he desired; and

*White Eagle was speaking of the early twentieth-century physicist and Spiritualist pioneer, Sir Oliver Lodge.

there was nothing left which could please or satisfy him. One day he came face to face with a wise man, a sage, who could see that his younger brother was troubled and unhappy, so he asked what was the matter. The man said that he was weary of life and sick in mind and soul. The sage promised him that if he was prepared to face tests, to go through ordeals, he would help him out of his despondency and into a new life. He pointed to the mountains in the distance and said to the man, 'Look at those sunlit heights. If you would find happiness and truth, satisfaction and peace of soul, you will have to climb those golden heights'.

The man realized what an enormous task lay before him. He went home and thought over the sage's words. We have not time to relate the whole story, but after a long journey our friend reached those golden heights and there he found companions of his spirit—those who had journeyed the same way as he. On those heights he found a life of perfection and beauty and was relieved of the sorrow and suffering which had been his on the plains and in the valleys. Because he found so much, in the end he had only one wish left: to return the way he had come in order to help his brothers and sisters on the plains to travel the same road and to reach those heights of happiness which had been his.

Those golden heights are waiting for you, along with every other soul; but first you must cast out false values and recognize that the most important thing in life is the awakening of the spirit of God within your own heart. You have to admit the profound and eternal truth that you are not limited by earthly things; you are not merely living for an allotted span on a material plane of existence. You are spirit; and as spirit, you are a daughter or a son of God. As a child of God you can claim your birthright—which is the power of the spirit within to free you from bondage in a material world.

You will say, 'That is all very well, but we are born into a material world, and must live by its laws'. You are both right and wrong, my friends. It is true that you are born into flesh, but you are spirit; and you are so placed that your spirit may quicken and grow and become conscious of its divine inheritance. You are not limited by the earth life. Many millions on this earth actually think that when their body dies, they die too! What a surprise they will have when they see the body lying inert and dead, and they themselves are still consciously living, although they have no power to raise their dead body! The spirit is thus set free in a world of spirit which immediately surrounds the earth plane.

So much depends upon you—upon you who have a little knowledge of spiritual things. You not only help yourself by good resolutions and aspirations, you help the whole world incarnate—and, too, the worlds around you, the worlds of discarnate souls. Your little light, which you show in the darkness of earth, can attract millions of disembodied souls who will learn from you if you are strong and resolute in spirit and keep your vision upon the heights. The world of tomorrow will be built upon the resolutions, aspirations and determinations of humanity today; and if that world is to be all you hope for, then it can only come if you declare yourself strong in the spirit, and are strong in the light of the Cosmic Christ which is both within and without you.

We have spoken of the millions of disembodied souls who are attracted to this earth. Do not imagine for one instant that all these souls are unevolved. On the contrary, there are many groups and companies of disembodied souls which are generally known as the brothers and sisters of the light, the company of the Star Brotherhood. *These are they which came out of great tribulation, and have washed their robes, and made them white in the blood of the Lamb.* They have found the worthlessness of materialism. They have climbed the mountain path and reached the peaks. They know now what lies before all men and women who have the will to build their lives upon spiritual realities and spiritual principles.

My brethren, only when these spiritual principles are put into practice everywhere will the golden age ever come. Such an age will not be founded upon material and scientific achievement, but by the simple and gentle of heart. It will be founded by those souls who have learned discernment, and who can see that any advancement is preceded by a developing spiritual outlook among human kind. The narrow outlook of an over-powerful and destructive intellect can only bring the world—or at least the humanity living upon that world—to utter chaos.

Your only way is the way of the spirit. We who have traversed the road know something of the truth; and we tell you that the path of the spirit lies immediately before you. Do not lay aside spiritual things, saying, 'It is all right; I know I am going to live on after my body is dead; I am going to a beautiful place. That is all that matters. I am not concerned with these people who are so quarrelsome. I will go my way, not theirs.' You cannot think in this way; you cannot live a life centred upon personal enjoyment while around you men and women are suffering. However obscure you feel yourself to be, you must be true to the spirit of Christ within: true to love and goodwill and brotherhood. You must tread the path of the spirit and you must aspire every moment to a more spiritual life. Do not wrap your robes around you as the Pharisees did, but be filled with sympathy and understanding for humanity and humanity's need.

While the new age of Aquarius will bring human kind opportunities, humanity can either use or abuse these opportunities. This statement applies to every individual soul, as well as to the world as a whole. You have to work for happiness, and for the blessings which the law of God is showering upon humanity. The great thing in this new age is going to be a parallel development of both the human and the divine nature; the human being and the divine being. You will have already noticed that powerful mental development has its dangers; side by side with this development there will be the opportunity for great spiritual unfoldment. Thus the first thing to be attained by men and women in this new age will be self-realization: realization of their own soul powers, their own spiritual powers.

We repeat, you are both divine and human. Neither aspect must be neglected. It is of utmost importance that the human side of the nature should be utilized in the right and true way as well as the divine nature, which also must be encouraged to grow in stature. The master Jesus came during the last age, the Piscean Age, to give humanity this clear teaching. He came representing both the human and the divine being. Here was the one who could enter into the sorrows and joys of his brothers and sisters; here was the one who found in the simple things his greatest joy; here was the man who worked in the fields, not like a beast of burden, but as a son of God, with his face towards the sun; and whose joy was to serve life, to serve God, to serve his brother–sister. This brings his divinity right through his human nature.

You must have that wonderful blending of the two. This will not happen all at once. There is a great deal of soul work to be done before humanity can demonstrate the qualities of the Aquarian Age. To you who listen, we say how lovely it will be; but all things of this nature have to be earned, and men and women have to learn in this new age the art of giving of themselves. Hold the picture before you of the life of the master Jesus, and you will see he gave himself without measure. The whole race will have to do likewise in the Aquarian Age if it wishes to enjoy the gifts which are waiting in the invisible for people to bring forth into the visible. You must therefore learn to give yourself without stint. This does not mean that you have to crucify yourself, but rather that you surrender the selfish demands of the mortal personality, and learn to see things in a truer perspective. You have to develop discernment, discrimination between what is worthwhile and what is worthless. You have to choose the better way—the narrow path—even though it does not appear so inviting.

Great changes come to humanity in the new age. The vibration of the earth is changing, the very substance of the earth and the physical body is changing. And those whose own soul vibrations are not sufficiently strong to withstand the more powerful vibrations of the earth, will be cared for, but they will sleep for a while, till the next great order sounds forth for the resurrection of the dead, or the sleeping. At the sound of the trumpet, they will rise from their sleep! The trumpet is the great sound which the initiate hears, which causes him or her to rise up from the tomb—the dense earthly conditions of life. It is the rising from the dead, from the tomb of materialism.

In the ushering-in of the Aquarian Age, the age of the great spirit of love and brotherhood, remember the mercy of God. If you play your part as it is shown to you, and strive always to be tolerant, and trust in God and God's mercy, you will then become an ever more pure and great channel for the mighty flood of the Christ love and light which is even now descending upon you all. For now, at this very moment, the Christ power is baptizing the earth, and wounds are being healed.

As you face this new age, we who work so closely with humanity pray that men and women will at last awaken to the truth of their being and to the purpose of their life here. Men and women are brought into contact with the physical plane in order that they may learn, and in order that they may experience joy and happiness to the highest degree possible on this earth. People are not born to suffer. We say that unreservedly. Each one of you was created to know joy and happiness. There is only one way in which joy and happiness can be attained, and that is by the way of spiritual realization. Such happiness is eternal; its duration is not for one life only.

You are pioneers. You are given an opportunity to help the younger brethren onward and upward to the golden heights. As you walk the earth life, hand in hand with your brother and sister (which means giving the hand of goodwill, helpfulness and sympathy in every material detail of life, we remind you), you are being guided and inspired and illumined by beings of former golden ages who now come to arouse and help humanity to go forth into the sunlight. May you all find happiness, serenity and a steady certainty.

What will the Aquarian Age be like?

Many beautiful qualities in human nature are going to be brought forth in this new age. Men and women are already beginning to extend their term of life in the physical body, and there will come a further prolongation. Life will become longer, because as each person evolves he or she will touch divine wisdom; though at first no-one will recognize having done so. This divine truth will percolate only slowly through to the mental body. The mental body will grow very powerful at the start of the new age, but human kind has arrived today at a certain point in its spiral of evolution where it is getting more spiritual balance, and so the destructive powers of the mind will after a while be held in check.

It is people like yourselves who are the pioneers of this new age. The powers behind the veil are looking to you and to other groups to bring to the earth this supreme light, this spiritual quality which must hold in its place the great mental power. We might almost describe the two (the spiritual strength and the mental power) as two opposites, which like force and energy are both necessary to the development and the keeping in place of physical matter.

Science, when wielded by the mind of the heart, will become a power for the blessing of human kind. Wonderful things are in store for the world when this blending, this balancing of the scientific mind with the spiritual mind, has been established. We can see into the future to a time when each man and woman has attained son–daughtership, by a process of self-mastery. We see a world made beautiful. We see cities built not only with material substance, but beautified by the light of the spirit, and this spiritual power harnessed to physical and material needs. We see graceful and spacious buildings, with light radiating from the walls of the room, from the ceilings, although there seems to be no-one particular point from which the light shines. This light will give warmth when necessary, but we also see that there will be a change in the climate.

Souls preparing for incarnation are now being so strengthened—by your help, if you are working for the light—that incoming personalities to your world, the newborn, will bring with them a memory of the beauty of the spirit worlds. In the new age buildings will become— shall we say?—as poems of beauty in stone. Beauty has already found expression in stone, do you not think, both in what is created today, and what was created in the past? Even the ruins which remain speak of grandeur and strength, but you have yet to see the delicacy, the beauty which can and will come. We look forward to the greater beauty of curves and beautiful lines in building. These will come with development of God-consciousness, when humanity begins to get beyond the mental plane to the celestial. Then will be brought through something of the beauty of the heavenly spheres.

Extremes of heat and cold will no longer exist, for the climate will be adjusted according to the needs of the people. This may sound to you like a fairy story, but if you will develop your inner vision you will begin to realize the possibilities for human kind as the spiritual power manifests more definitely. When spirit becomes dominant in matter you will see the results in all forms of life, in all the arts and the sciences and in the lives of people themselves.

With the Aquarian Age you will see a revolution in education, in religion, in science. Instead of education being a process of intensive mental study, so that the mind becomes blocked and stuffy, the new influences will penetrate the spirit; and the intuition of the children will be unfolded and stimulated by vibrations of beauty, of colour, and art and form. On the etheric plane are grand libraries in which the soul can search. It will be possible for you to do this in the Aquarian Age. Instead of a process of cramming, education will be so applied that it will strike into the very innermost part of the soul and will open out and bring forth knowledge which is within. Make no mistake, knowledge and wisdom come primarily from within, and with the right process, with the correct motive and aspiration, the soul can unfold the fruits of all knowledge and wisdom.

May we tell you, also, of the part music and speech are going to play in the future? Even now the stimulation in people of the love of music has begun. The power of music is going to increase. Beauty itself is going to increase. More beautiful music will stimulate the mental qualities and will gently open the heart centre. That music is coming, and will raise the vibrations of the earth. It will have a great effect upon the soul-development of the race, and those beautiful buildings that are suitable and have the right acoustics will be used, and the music will be sent forth from such places into human life. Music is a tool, an avenue, a channel through which these great spiritual forces will flow to human kind, stimulating again, in turn, the sleeping powers latent in every human being.

Music is beautiful architecture. Music is beautiful art, for music produces colours more exquisite than you have ever seen. The use of the throat centre, the use of speech, is of great importance. Beautiful language has a part to play in the new age in the building-up of constructive good.

Spiritual language is a common language. In the higher spheres there is just one language. In time unification of all the races on earth will necessarily bring one common language of the spirit, which will be interpreted in the same speech through the lips.

The ear will be trained to hear beautiful music, the eye to see beauty. There will be beauty expressed throughout life ... beauty ... the external expression of the spirit; beauty, not the creation of the intellect alone, but in itself an expression of the divine.

Movement, speech and music are all connected with ritual, and ritual is connected with the utilization of invisible forces. When speech is correctly used it means that invisible forces are gathered up and built into form, or are directed to a certain centre or place on the physical plane. This certainly has an influence, for it is a creative power. Speech is a great agent for the control of occult force.

Dancing, of course, was much used in the temples of the past. If you could see clairvoyantly what takes place with the movement of a trained dancer who is working from the spirit and not only from the mind, you would see most beautiful designs of light. Everywhere the dancer went they would create forms, and you would see all these forms built into the ether; you would see them being built of light. Forms built of light in the higher ether will, in due time, gradually crystallize, and be brought through into matter. Movement will have a great deal to do in the new age, not only with the body itself, with the prolongation of life and health, but also with the creation and re-creation of life. Movement and speech are very important. You may be amused but this is all part of spiritual development.

Works of art will become living creations, and the vibrations of nature will be so heightened, so quickened, and the gardeners will be so trained by the human creative spirit, that the gardens will be beauty enshrined. You raise the question: 'Can we improve on nature?'. With pure spirit functioning through the mind of God's highest creation on earth—the human—beauty will be expressed in the arrangement and control of nature. We speak with knowledge; we know of that which we have seen in the higher worlds. We know that nature, as you see it on earth, is not yet perfect; but with men and women working harmoniously with nature, there will come further unfoldment. We see indeed a beautiful earth!

The Seventh Ray

You may have heard a certain amount about the seventh ray, which is particularly coming into operation in the Aquarian Age.* The seventh ray is considered the ray of ritual, ceremonial, brotherhood and the higher psychic development; we will call it the ray of beauty. In other words, it is the age for the development of inner powers, soul powers; but the seventh-ray work is taking other forms too on the material plane. It is connected, for instance, with the development of physical science. The seventh ray is guarded, protected by the wise ones acting under divine wisdom and power. In order to assist the true unfoldment of human spiritual power and the right application of science, both psychic, spiritual and material, it is necessary that each soul's knowledge should be balanced by the indwelling spirit of the Lord Christ.

The age of Aquarius is the age of the mind, a mental age; yet it is both a scientific and a spiritual age. While men and women are treading this difficult path, which is like a razor's edge, they will come up against many difficult situations not only in individual, but in national and communal life. The conscious unity of the human with the divine spirit is the foundation of everything. We of the Brotherhood of the Star return to you for one purpose—in order to help you to awaken to the knowledge of spiritual life, and the brotherhood of all life. This means the awakening of the vision, of the soul or psyche to the spiritual or inner worlds: to worlds of light, happiness and harmony, which is what God intended human life to enjoy. In this life of the perfected being we see, shining above the great company of brethren in the heavens, the

*The seven-ray system is clearly set out by White Eagle in WALKING WITH THE ANGELS (White Eagle Publishing Trust, 1998)

blazing Christ Star: the symbol of the Christ man–woman. The spiritual power descending into humanity is symbolised by the triangle with the point coming down and perfectly interpenetrating and balancing human nature. The human being is made perfect by the Christ birth, the greatest thing that can ever happen on this planet. You will see this becoming ever clearer with the progress of all seventh-ray things—with the development of spiritual science and the awakening of the human consciousness.

Revolution or Evolution?

There will be many unexpected happenings in the new age. Miracles, my children, the world will call them. From many quarters a flash of light will come to illumine the darkness of the earth. The effect will be like a revolution, but not of the kind you think—a revolution of thought and ideas, which are going to flood in before very long.

The truth of the Brotherhood of the ancient wisdom and of the White Light, established long ago, will be re-established on your earth. Groups will be formed all over the world, and even the governments of the nations will be formed of men and women initiated into the ancient brotherhood of the light of the Son–Daughter of God. The wisdom from the East will be established in the West, to work on the outer planes, on governments, and in the commercial world. It sounds impossible for the spirit of the Son of God to be established in the commercial world, but it will be so. Instead of competition there will be cooperation and brotherhood, and the goodwill which is to come in the age of Aquarius.

In the new age, human kind will no longer be satisfied with any church that dictates a policy which gives it power over the people. Indeed, the individual will no longer want a church to interpret truth for him or her. People will permit no barrier to stand between them and their Lord. Each will become his or her own priest, his or her own interpreter; and human kind will regain the wisdom of the ages, the wisdom it had in the ancient days of the Lost Continents. People will understand the ancient wisdom and use its laws for their own government.

They will apply these laws to their commerce and to every detail of their daily round and common task. Life will be founded upon spirit, while the people will live and worship in the spirit of brotherhood. Old and outworn creeds and dogmas will pass into nothingness and be forgotten. 'Churchianity' will crumble away. Even the form of governments to which humanity has clung for centuries will die out, and it will be government for all—and not for protecting the rights of a few—by a government under direction from the council chamber of the cosmic hierarchies. This method of guiding and inspiring the leaders of all the nations with the ideal of goodwill, with the ideal of the good in the whole of humanity, is in course of preparation and will lead to a universal brotherhood of individuals and of nations.

Great changes come. Keep calm, simple and humble, and give from your hearts the truest brotherhood you understand, and you will assist not in revolution, but in steady, progressive evolution.

What comes before this? Will the Uranian influence of Aquarius cause floods and earthquakes, and the sweeping away of that which is unwanted in the new age? Or will that which appears useless be woven into its fabric? So much depends upon the response of those who are now living on earth and who understand. What a responsibility is yours! You are builders—master masons—and your Master, the Grand Architect, has issued his orders, not through the lips of any human being, but through the heart. Within the heart, through the sufferings and restrictions brought by the influence of Saturn, the password is sounded which flings wide the gateway into the age of Aquarius.

There must come cataclysms, not necessarily of a physical nature, but perhaps through the soul of things changing—a revolution which will not necessarily cause bloodshed, but a revolution of thought. The human spirit will rise up and say: 'We cannot slay our brother–sister.' The whole being will rebel against war. Already we see the influence of the new age creeping into the hearts of people, demanding that there shall be peace, equality, brotherhood, the right to express the spirit and to live harmoniously, freely, to worship God in their own true way. Slowly into people's hearts is creeping the spirit which says: 'There are other worlds beyond the material world; there are other ideals to live for beyond the accumulation of material wealth and power—which fades in time and leaves behind only dust and ashes.'

The White Rose

Visualize a temple—a small, circular white temple with a domed roof, set in a beautiful woodland estate. In the centre of this temple is a small altar; and upon the altar is a perfect white flower. It is pure white, and the petals are open to receive the rays of the sun, which pour between the pillars supporting the dome. This temple is known as the temple of peace. It is more real, more solid and eternal than any buildings on your earth plane. Those will crumble and pass away, but spiritual temples are eternal like the Cosmos.

The flower of peace upon the altar is sending forth a very beautiful perfume. As you receive wafts of this perfume through your spiritual senses, it stimulates the sense of peace in your soul, and that is projected again into the atmosphere. The soul is creating the perfume of peace, a reservoir of peace which is constantly added to; and equanimity is thus breathed into the world. Angels use this perfume, with the intent of permeating the hearts of those who hold positions of state.

The white rose—symbol of purity, pure love—is the symbol of John, the one who is working most closely with Jesus; a symbol of a part or an aspect of the dual soul of Jesus. The symbol of the white rose inspires pure love, divine love, within you. The white rose and the red rose are two symbols of life, the white rose being pure spirit; and the red rose being the spirit or human soul after it has passed through deep human experiences.

So many of you are struggling and suffering great sorrow; enduring many trials and difficulties. Yet all the problems of sickness and want and poverty (and even the problems of wealth) can be solved, if only humanity will give themselves to studying, to endeavouring to understand, the law of love.

What a time is this for hope! What do you hope for? All kinds of things. You are hoping that human kind will awaken from its nightmare and see the true purpose of living. You are hoping, as you do at the end of winter, that very soon the bright days of spring will come along; that soon the buds will break and the green leaves open. Why do you hope? Because you have confidence in nature. Why do you hope human kind will awaken from its nightmare and seek to establish brotherhood and goodwill on earth? Because you know that in every man and woman is a divine spark. Hope is confidence in the invisible power and confidence in God.

In the autumn you are able to see little brown swellings on every twig. At the end of winter they are bursting, and show little green shoots. This gives you hope for longer days; bloom on trees and fruit; hope for a harvest before next winter. You have confidence in a God who thus brings the divine life-force through into physical manifestation, even as God brought forth into physical manifestation the Son of God. You can see this very simply expressed in men and women who may tell you they have neither faith, nor hope. Yet they are kind to one another. Such kindness is an expression of Christ. This gives us all hope that this shining, eternal Presence will become manifest on earth.

Is it the second coming of Christ that we foresee? Do we see the little buds, the green shoots of kindness breaking forth in human kind now, so that we may hope the world will be raised up to Christ? He came to teach the one supreme truth (which the world has still to learn) of brotherhood and love. Only love can bring to you—individually—happiness; and God intends His–Her children to realize happiness.

When love comes into the heart it causes an illumination. This can actually be seen by spirit helpers as a light. Where love has entered, a man or woman looks like a little torch. Love brings illumination and light. When love comes in entirety into the human family, there will be so many lights that the fog will disappear. Then we shall see each other, as St Paul says, not *through a glass, darkly, but then face to face*; and we shall know, as we are known.

VI

RELIGION: A UNIVERSAL BROTHER–SISTERHOOD

For where two or three are gathered together in my name, there am I in the midst of them.

Matthew 18 : 20

I, if I be lifted up, will draw all men unto me.

John 12 : 32

I AM THAT I AM.

Exodus 3 : 14

I am Alpha and Omega, the beginning and the ending, saith the Lord.

Revelation 1 : 8

Ye cannot serve God and mammon.

Matthew 6 : 24

And, behold, the veil of the temple was rent in twain from the top to the bottom.

Matthew 27 : 51

And God shall wipe away all tears from their eyes; and there shall be no more death, neither sorrow, nor crying, neither shall there be any more pain: for the former things are passed away.

Revelation 21 : 4

Where there is no vision, the people perish.

Proverbs 29 : 18

This is my commandment, That ye love one another, as I have loved you.

John 15 : 12

IT IS IN the plan of the Infinite Wisdom, we have told you, that there shall be at this time a special outpouring of the light upon humanity, so that humanity can speed up its own spiritual evolution. There was a similar stimulation of the human spirit nearly two thousand years ago, at the beginning of the age of Pisces. Much work has to be done, and much which is unwanted has to be cleaned away. Sometimes the cleansing process is painful, for it means a breaking-up of old, outworn conditions. All have to go. You must be prepared for this process at the commencement of the new age, and you can then welcome new ways of life, new religions, new methods in healing, new ideas in literature, art and music.

We would lift you out of the little box you call mind. We would raise you to the infinite or divine mind, which is quite different from the mind which functions through the lower mental plane. We want you to rise above all the old creeds and dogmas of the past: they have served as stepping stones, but they must no longer obstruct. For a new interpretation is being sent to you: maybe it is the Spirit of truth which the Master promised.

For two thousand years orthodox Christianity has been built or founded upon faith, and we fear that the letter has obliterated the spirit. It is like a temple or cathedral constructed with beautiful windows, but without light shining behind them to illuminate the beauty of the building. Now the human spirit is ready to receive the light, the true light of

Christ; and this light is coming onto the earth plane now. It is coming like a searchlight. It is going to illumine the cathedral of the Christian church or Christ's church. It will illumine all the churches and places of religion. All barriers and prejudices of mind—pride—will be swept away, for the religion of the future will not be a religion of faith and belief, it will be a religion of life and reality. It will revolutionize every thought and act of human life. It is a new church or brotherhood which comes, built not upon the work of people but upon the work of John the Beloved—St John. There are groups under the name of John who come to people on earth, those who have opened the mind and have brought the cup to be filled with the living wine of Christ. And so you shall see on the earth plane a great universal brotherhood: one church—the mystical church of John the Divine. It is these brothers and sisters you are already contacting in the spheres of truth.

When men and women are ready, the ancient temples will be re-built. By this we mean not the actual physical temples, but that the mystery schools of the past will come again to the earth. This is how the universal brotherhood of the spirit will be established upon earth....

Some people from the Piscean Age have responded already to the intuitional influence (the influence of Neptune and Uranus). This is the influence which will be for the sustenance of humanity and usher in the age of the spirit, the age when the human spirit will function freely and consciously in higher worlds, while still in contact with the flesh. Now you are on the cusp of the Aquarian Age, and are receiving certain stimulation from the Aquarian teachers and masters. The result will be that in the new age religion will take an entirely different form. It will not be the old priesthood, the orthodox form of worship. It will be a religion which will help each man and woman to develop the God within him- or herself; and each of you will learn that the best way to stimulate this divine power within is through group work. A few will be drawn together. *Where two or three are gathered together in my name there will I be in their midst,* said Christ through the master Jesus. Religion will take the form of group work: in other words, its form will be that of true brotherhood of the spirit. Some lower aspects of brotherhood are being forced upon the world today: powerful and dominating leaders, seeming to speak with the ideal of brotherhood, are forcing ideas upon people, ideas that later become all the more distorted. Younger souls seize upon such ideas of freedom without having the deeper knowledge and wisdom to comprehend the divine truth that brotherhood must be of the spirit, and the spirit teaches men and women to respect their brothers and sisters, to revere the dignity of human life, human work, and human worship.

This is the true form of brotherhood which will come from the heaven world, through spiritual rays stimulating the human heart centre. Men and women will then look out upon the world with broad and humane vision. As we have said, they will have a great love of beauty; a love of the arts and music, and all things which will help them to develop soul-powers; and they will have a vision open to the inner, to the spiritual planes of life. They will learn that thought is a very powerful tool of the master mason.

You are already beginning to have some idea of the power of thought. When the Aquarian Age becomes really established, men and women will be very careful how they use their thought-power, because they will learn that they can manipulate etheric substance with their thought. In this manner, they will come into the occult realms of life and begin to understand ceremonial magic and true ritual.

Developing the Feeling Nature

The world is advancing, even though this advance may not be apparent to you who are blindfolded and have only a partial revelation of what is happening either in your own life or in the collective life of the world. What distorts your vision is the mind of earth, which judges from its own low level. This mind of earth has no power to see the gradual impregnation by divine spirit of the soul, the soul either of the individual or of the earth itself.

This soul of the earth is created by pain and travail. You may not agree because you do not comprehend the full meaning of what is called pain. Pain is joy. You can feel pain with exceeding joy. Do you not know the exquisite feeling of joy which is pain to you? Great happiness, exceeding happiness can be painful. Pain and joy are akin to each other, being two separate aspects of the same thing, being light and shade, both springing from the same principle. Through the human being undergoing pain the soul goes through its formation, and is strengthened and built up.

Once you know this you will not shrink from any experience. You will learn to welcome pain when once you understand what pain can do, what pain actually is. For pain is creating, is beautifying the soul by developing the power to feel; developing intuition, that sixth sense which will become universal in the new age, and will give vision into other worlds, and will bring through into the mind of earth, into the outer self, a consciousness of truths of universal, of heavenly life.*

The individual cannot find God by intellect alone. People are trying so to do at the present time, however. Many are seeking to intellectualize God; but no-one, we repeat, can find God through the intellect alone. Everyone has to go through a development of their soul, their feelings and their love first. You can only lastingly find God through life, through your feelings, through your soul; so that the soul becomes like a bridge between heaven and earth, bringing humanity back again to God.

The soul is the bridge. It enables the child of earth to contact God again. We are trying to convey the nature of this divine Trinity of Father, Mother and Son, the perfect and holy Trinity of life. We are endeavouring to show the necessity for that marriage or union between spirit and soul to take place within every human being.

It is the woman aspect, the Divine Mother aspect, which is the tenderness, the love and the gentleness in life, the tenderness without which spiritual death must ensue. Do you see the importance of woman's place in the scheme of things? First let us say that women, those who are in the highly-privileged position on earth of being in a woman's body with womanly qualities, have great responsibilities. They do not all recognize

*See Chapter X, 'The Age of Intuition'

such responsibilities, for they allow their lower or weaker self to take possession of them instead of realizing their noble and divine attribute, the attribute of the Divine Mother. The work of the woman in you—whether you are physically a mother or not in this world—is to give love and motherhood, to mother all life; to express motherhood with tender love and sympathy—and with wisdom, which is as important as the love. Finding the woman within you, you must endeavour to develop the qualities of the Divine Mother. Can you see that the Divine Mother is herself the soul of humanity? It is the soul, and the soul is the intermediary between the individual self and the First Principle or Will of God.

When you arise and manifest the dignity of the divine principle that is behind womanhood, wars will cease because the soul (or the woman) desires neither strife nor war. The soul is peace-loving; the soul yearns for beauty, harmony and perfection; the soul, being intuitive, can look into the future desiring to protect the race, not to destroy it. We speak most earnestly to all women, urging them to develop the qualities of the noble, the holy Mary, the mother aspect.

With the blending of soul and spirit the perfect being is born, the one who is capable of taking the Christ initiation, who is capable of crucifying the lower self, crucifying matter, dispensing with the lower form of matter. You do not understand what this means yet, but we will just say at this moment that the crucifixion of matter, the dispensing with matter, means that a time will come when the Christ child, born from the two great Principles of Life, will rule matter, will rule the earth, and its darkness will be no more. For the earth's vibrations will become so etherealized, so harmonized that it will be a world of light.

A New Heaven and a New Earth

The religion brought to the earth millions of years ago is a religion not on the lips but in the heart. We see in the future temples or sanctified places to which the new brotherhoods are drawn: shall we say sanctified centres of grace and power, wherein men and women can worship their Father–Mother God?—not with lips, but with the outpouring of hearts, and the drawing to themselves of creative forces, and the utilization of those forces for the gradual perfecting or growth of all forms of life.

But there is much more than this. There will come the drawing of those forces beyond the earth plane to help the evolving life upon other planets in due time. This seems far off and impossible to you, no doubt. The idea of a new church gives us a sense of limitation, even of suffocation. We hope we offend no-one. But we would speak of a brotherhood of men and women and an outpouring, a truer communion with Christ. We think of an intermingling of Christ with His–Her people on earth.

The second coming! We see the raising up of the people. If I be raised up, said Jesus—if the Christ within be raised up—*I will draw all men unto me!* When the Christ within all people is raised up, and they worship in spirit and in true action and in daily service, then in themselves they must be raised up.

The truths taught long ago by Jesus, and so beautifully written down by John, have to be known and lived. They have not been so lived except by a few saints. Even these saints were limited by the world of their day. Now we are coming to a new age, and these same teachings of John are going to found a new church, but not a church such as you know today. The church of St John will be built into people's lives, into their hearts, into their souls. Each person will learn to worship in his or her own temple—that is, in the sacred place of the heart. People will not live by physical values only, but by the light of their own spirit, and their own spirit will show them how to behave towards their companions. There will not be the need then for social legislation. The foundations of the church of St John will be laid on pure spirit. The cathedral will be raised out of people's lives. On earth will come the spirit of perfect brotherhood. Then people will no longer foolishly worship Mammon. The prince of this world will recede and fall away before the spirit of love and brotherhood. *I AM THAT I AM.* 'I AM the divine flame', says the Christ.

In the Aquarian Age you will find this consciousness of the living Christ fully developed in people and on earth. There will be no more slaughter, no shedding of blood, innocent or guilty, but an intermingling with all planes of spiritual life. In the Gospel story, when Jesus was crucified, the veil of the temple was rent in two—a symbolic portrayal of what one day will take place. The rending of the veil is the intermingling of those higher or spiritual planes of life with the physical planes. Human kind will open its eyes to the glories of heaven. There will be no more separation. *And I saw a new heaven and a new earth.* There shall be no more gnashing of teeth! The terror and sorrow and sickness to which the flesh seems heir, will be overcome, will lie as dust; for by the birth, the resurrection of the Christ within, human kind will have entered into the kingdom of the loving God and all limitations will have passed away.

Hold to your Dreams

Many grumblers think that the golden age is just a dream. Dreams—as we in spirit very well know, so we can speak from experience—actually create external conditions. *Where there is no vision the people perish!* So hold to your dreams and keep on keeping on. You will always be hearing from us: keep on keeping on. So many cannot do this. They go to sleep by the wayside. They get discouraged. They turn back. But the soul who perseveres and keeps on keeping on reaches the goal of spiritual liberation.

People find it such a temptation—it is much easier to do—to go here, there, everywhere; going to all kinds of places: to the west, to the east, to the south, in search of a master! And all the time the Master is within, so close to them! Nearer than breathing, closer than hands and feet. This is simple truth. You will find nothing more beautiful than what you can find in your own inner temple. As you learn to seek this serenity, this peace, this tranquillity—as you learn in humility to kneel before the communion table—so you will find the greatest treasure, the perfect gift. Be brave and keep on with courage, and keep before you the golden light towards which you are ever moving.

There is so much that can be said, but remember these points: you are on the cusp of the Aquarian Age. The symbol for the Aquarian Age is both the white eagle and the figure who carries the water pot, the divine waters. In the new age, religion will come from the heart and every one of you will learn to unfold your own God-qualities and God-powers. Until you have unfolded these qualities you cannot be entrusted with the greater knowledge. Hence the teaching of the master Jesus, which was so clear, so emphatic, and which the world still ignores: *Love one another*. Until each of you can love your neighbour, you cannot receive the wisdom of the gods. So the Piscean Age was to teach human beings the value of a good life, a pure life, in preparation for the next age of Aquarius: which is going to put into their hands very great powers, of the mind and the heart. Human beings must be led to use those powers for constructive purposes and for the upliftment of the whole human race.

VII

THE AGE OF THE SPIRIT

Before Abraham was, I am.

John 8 : 58

Master, carest thou not that we perish?

Mark 4 : 38

I am the way, the truth and the life.... Believe me that I am in the Father and the Father in me.... I will not leave you comfortless: I will come to you.

John 14 : 6, 11, 18

I am the resurrection, and the life.

John 11 : 35

And as Moses lifted up the serpent in the wilderness, even so must the Son of man be lifted up: That whosoever believeth in him should not perish, but have everlasting life.

John 3 : 14–15

They shall beat their swords into ploughshares, and their spears into pruninghooks.

Isaiah 2 : 4

THE SPECIAL outpouring of power from the spiritual Sun, of which we speak, comes at the close of a spiritual cycle. At the end of each two thousand years a happening occurs cosmically, and there is a conjunction between the earthly sun and that spiritual sphere of light which is animating the sun, and all life on earth. The power which is poured out was known to the ancients as the solar force.

The ancient Sun-gods were like giants, half as tall again as the average person of today. Full of the glory of the sun, they were beautiful to look upon, their most striking feature being their eyes, which shone with the glory of the spiritual Sun. These God–men and God–women— beings of the Sun, they could be called—possessed the secrets of the solar force, and their work was to teach the young souls as they came into incarnation concerning the secrets of life; and as we have just said, some of these young souls used the secrets unwisely, bringing about the downfall of themselves and others and the disruption of the earth.

As human kind drew deeper into heavier and denser physical matter, men and women became concerned only with their physical appetites, losing contact with angelic beings and the Sun-beings and almost losing contact with the solar force: almost, but not entirely. The secrets of the solar force were very jealously guarded. The only way this knowledge could be passed down through the ages was through the initiates or the sages. If you study the ancient philosophers with a certain amount of understanding and knowledge, you will recognize in their teaching knowledge of the solar force. Had the masses possessed the knowledge, or the power which the knowledge would give, they would have destroyed themselves. For all that (you may know from legend), there have been occasions when the mysteries became known to certain priests who were not strong and pure in love, and these priests conveyed the mysteries in the wrong way to others. Then the power, the solar force, was used destructively. This was not intended at first, but when an individual's lower self was not under control it rose in selfish desire for power over other human beings.

A few centuries ago there came to Europe a revival of what is known as Masonic teaching. The old secrets were embodied again in Masonry but they were referred to as the 'lost' secrets. They have become lost today, because humanity has enclosed itself in dark earthliness and has been too much concerned with its own selfish existence—not a wicked life necessarily, but an ignorant one. Ignorance has enfolded women and men. Fortunately, the secrets have never been wholly lost, because God has never left humanity without a witness. *I will not leave you comfortless.* These same secrets, which in the past were spoken, transferred, imparted to the brethren by initiates, teachers and sages, concern not only the high initiates and priests of ancient cults, but men and women today. Enslaved by materialism, humanity has until recently been like a prisoner bound hand and foot and unable to rise by its own power, being dependent upon brothers and sisters of the spirit to assist it to rise.

Only a century or so ago, the brotherhood in spirit who watch over the progress of people on earth planned to send them a key which would enable those of steady heart to unlock a door which would lead them on to a path of light. We are referring to the introduction of what is known as modern Spiritualism. Its object has been to break up the dark cloak which hung round humanity. The initiates decided that the time had come for the veil which hung between the two states of existence to be lifted. Simple people started to experience psychic demonstrations, their experiences pointing to the fact that there were unseen human intelligences with power to communicate. From that time the veil began to thin between the two states of life.

This was the way chosen by the Masters of the Wisdom to put into the hands of individual men and women the key which unlocked the door leading to a path of light. If it was patiently and wisely followed, this path would enable them step by step to shed the dense clothing in which they were wrapped. By this we mean the clothing first of all of the Earth, then of the Water element, then of the Air element. Finally, people would be ready to receive the full power of the Fire element, which is the divine fire or the solar force. Man–woman would be able to unveil Godlike potentialities, not only in actions but in knowledge. The earthly being would learn how his or her higher vehicles functioned. Each man or woman would learn how to direct the solar force right through the physical being and through his or her own self direct it to the earth.

The urgency for spiritual wisdom and love to be imparted and unfolded in each human being is extreme. First of all, though, the doctrine of Christ must be imparted more clearly. People—scientists particularly—have to recognize the place in the scheme of things of the Christ life, if as a race they are to be saved from self-destruction. Have no fear, my children, about this. Do not allow yourselves to fear, because if you do you will be going over to the enemy (not that we quite like the word): you will be going over to the negative forces. You will perhaps glimpse how gravely significant it is for the gospel of wisdom, love and knowledge to be imparted, so that step by step you may advance into the Temple of the Mysteries.

Although you do not realize it, you are surrounded at all times by a vast company of spirit beings. You possess certain vehicles or bodies through which you can make contact with the different planes. Your physical body enables you to contact physical matter. As we have already said, the majority of humanity are only concerned with their physical bodies. This body is not the only vehicle in which you can function. Each human being has, within, the four elements—Earth, Water, Air and Fire—and has separate bodies or vehicles through which those worlds can be contacted.

The Solar Force

The solar force, the sun power, is directly connected with the world of Fire and also with the heart and with the human spirit. It is the cohesive power holding all life together. It is the pivot, first of the greater universe and then of the smaller universe of humanity. We put it to you that it is the spirit of Christ: it is the sun within; and the sun within manifests in human life as human love, human kindness. As it unfolds it manifests with greater power. You know it by various names. Shall we call it tonight the power of the I AM? You remember the quotation: *Before Abraham was, I AM.* The Son of God; the Son of the Father–

Mother; the I AM; the solar force; the Sun-light; the love within the human soul. The love within the human soul is the same power that can create universes. In the individual it can transform a life from darkness to light. You can witness it for yourselves very simply. Look carefully at those of your friends whom you know are following the inner path of Christ. You are aware of their aura of light, power, peace and tranquillity. That is a manifestation—in perhaps a minor degree, and maybe even a major degree—of this solar force.

Solar force is also the healing power. You can depend upon the guides, upon the healers and the angels, to bring you healing power, when you realize that within you is the sun and centre of that force. You will then become not only healers of sick bodies but healers of nations, healers of life—animal life, vegetable life, physical life—and then healers of the soul and the mind, because this solar force works through all the planes surrounding the earth and the bodies surrounding the physical body.

The Water element is concerned with the emotions and passions, and you will realize how important it is for Water to be under control, under the command of the Master. Hence the parable—do you remember it?—of the boat being tossed on the lake. The disciples were fearful. They were seeking their Master, remember, just as you may be disciples seeking your master. When you become storm-tossed by fear, anxiety and passion, the divine power, the force which should control you, is sleeping. The disciple calls, '*Master, carest thou not that we perish?*'. You call in your daily lives, 'I am afraid'. Everything is tumbling around you. The boat of your soul rocks in a great storm. When the soul calls rightly the Master hears. In you rises the divine power which causes you to be still, to be tranquil. Be at peace. Your Master takes over control of your boat—which is your soul—and you become calm.

Do you now see the true meaning of Christ being the saviour of human kind? It is not the fact of a physical body being nailed to a wooden cross which saves humanity from its sins, but you yourself when you rise (or go within) to that supreme plane of consciousness where you contact the solar force: your solar self, the Christ. The Christ takes possession of all the vehicles and bodies. This is what salvation is—not the death of another human like yourselves on a cross, although that too has a wonderful symbolism.

Such symbols as these have been used all through the ages to convey to the human understanding the divine mysteries. Do you not see the way before you and the glory which awaits you? Even the bitterness and disappointment and frustration of your plans—all these things will be smoothed away and will be as nothing to you when you have caught the vision glorious.

This mystery teaching which we are imparting in a minor degree has existed over aeons of time. Great temples in remote parts of the world are mysteries to your investigators today, and they will remain mysteries until men and women learn the inner secret. When they become possessed of spiritual secrets, then they will understand the purpose of the temples of Egypt, Tibet, China, the Andes, Mexico, Atlantis. They will understand the purpose of the temples in Britain where the priests of the sun, the priests who had the wisdom of the solar force, worshipped and worked to control and direct the elements; and worshipped and worked to direct the great masses of beings belonging to those elements for the creation and the projection of a rich and beautiful life in a beautiful world. This is God's gift to humanity—God's plan for humanity—not the present state of greed and selfishness which exists. Can you not see that the only way for the true reform, for evolution to come, is not the way of rebellion and revolution amongst the masses and the nations, but the way of spiritual evolution? Then there will come true and lasting peace, and the golden age will be ushered in.

The Plumed Serpents

You will recognize, as time passes, the stimulation of humanity's spiritual powers. You will recognize the rising of the solar force both in men and women and in the earth itself. The purpose of human incarnation is to develop in each person the solar body, and to raise the solar force. This force is also referred to as the serpent fire—which dwells in the centre of kundalini. As a soul evolves that serpent turns its head upward, and will gradually, through stimulation of the sympathetic nervous system, cause the seven chakras in the etheric body to open. As this force arises and stimulates the centres, they open and become the windows of the soul. The solar force comes into a soul and shines forth through the chakras, developing that Christ power, that supreme heavenly light.

If you study the lives of the saints you will read of miraculous happenings. If you have knowledge of this serpent-power you will understand why these saints—some devoted to a wonderful life of contemplation, prayer and desire for union with God—seem at a certain stage to have had an inrush of miraculous power, so that miracles are recorded which no ordinary person can understand. Such things are left unexplained by the ordinary lower mind, but those who have begun to tread the upward path recognize in these happenings the arising of the solar force. By this same power the saints, the disciples, the prophets of the past have demonstrated to earthly men and women the reality of this supreme solar fire.

Can we illustrate this? You will remember the episode of Elijah being caught up in a chariot of fire to heaven.* That is how it looked to the onlookers. The inner truth was that he became so filled with solar force that he was raised from earth and carried up out of the sight of those who were watching. This is not impossible, and although it is called a miracle you will understand that these spiritual demonstrations are not in truth miraculous, but rather the natural outworking of the divine power when it uses the human form. This is what is to be expected, particularly in this age of Aquarius.

There will come to the earth a great baptism of this spiritual sun. There will come a great stimulation of the holy, the divine fire, the Christ spirit in the heart of all peoples. You may say, it is a long way ahead. You cannot be sure. We cannot; we do not know, but we do know the spiritual laws which govern life. We know that the law is for this serpent

*2 Kings 1 : 11–12

fire gradually to rise and illumine each person's mind and heart. In this we know God and all creatures.

Knowledge concerning this solar force, this serpent-power, has always existed. Throughout the scriptures you will find references to the serpent-power. Moses gave a clear indication of it when dealing with the children of Israel in the wilderness. Moses was an initiate of high degree. His very name means that: it originated from Osiris; that is, from the chief priest of the solar force. Moses was therefore a priest of the order of Osiris, which means of the order of Melchizedek.

When Moses led the children into the wilderness they became weary and started to grumble.* They were wandering in the same wilderness as we all do. Everyone on the path leading towards the light comes to a time of loneliness and desolation. You have all experienced such times. Then you wander in the desert, feeling very despondent and inclined to murmur and grumble.

The Israelites wandered in the wilderness for forty days or 'years', a period likened to the length of time the child in its mother's womb waits for birth. Those Israelites aspiring to reach the Promised Land were led to a place where all was barren and where they had no food but white manna from heaven. This white food is indicative of mental food, food that feeds the mental body, silver being the metal that signifies the intellect. Such food was not really satisfying to the children of Israel. They grew tired of it. They wanted something better but did not know what.

When at another time Moses came down from the mountain, from a state of higher consciousness, back to his pupils, he found that they had made for themselves a graven image. They were worshipping a golden calf.† This is indicative of the wrong use to which they were putting their newly-awakened, slightly-stimulated psychic and occult powers. When Moses descended, he saw the graven image and realized the misuse which his people had made of their knowledge. Is this not like all occultists who miss the way because they go so keenly for the

*Numbers 21 : 4–5   †Exodus 32

74

things of the mind and long to possess occult power that can so easily be put to wrong use?

Moses was very grieved. To deal with the grumbles and afflictions of his people he made a serpent out of brass and set it up upon a rod.* He taught the people in symbolic language that what they had to do was to raise this serpent-power to the highest part of their being, which is the heart and the head. Then they would receive divine illumination and be taken to the Promised Land. Do we make clear the wonderful meaning of this old scripture?—the teaching to the aspirant and to those who were ready, those who were eager to progress along the path of evolution, that they must not use the serpent-power for selfish ends or selfish gratification. It must be raised and worshipped as a holy and precious thing. Did not Jesus, years after, say, *Even so, must the Son of man be lifted up?*

Another way of looking at this would be to see it as referring to the serpent-power that has to be raised up into the head and the heart, so that each man and woman becomes not a person of earth but of eternal life. This is the coming of the supreme Sun-light, the life, in the form of Christ through Jesus. Although this light had been demonstrated through other initiates in the past, there came at this time a full manifestation of the Christ life. The solar body of Jesus had been brought to perfection. The Christ light manifested through him and spoke with clear and definite authority, saying, *I am the way, the truth and the life.* That was this solar force, this divine life which was speaking.

At other times, Jesus also gave teaching concerning eternal life: 'Unless you believe in me....' *Believe me that I am in the Father and the Father in me....* 'Believe on me and you shall be saved....' 'I come to give you life; I come to bring you out of darkness into light.' *I am the resurrection, and the life.* Do you not see, my children, in the death of the physical body the great promise of the coming of the solar being, the solar body? The physical, earthly body dies. Of course the lower aspect dies; but that supreme solar body which is being brought into being, which is creating and evolving, which is developing through all the incarnations of the soul

*Numbers 21 : 8–9

in the physical body, that is leading you eventually to eternal life.

You do not enter upon eternal life until the full consciousness of the Christ life is born in you, until you have developed your solar body. That body is only created when the force of which we speak is turned upward. This is the way that all men and women must tread. The Christ, speaking through Jesus, made it so plain: *Even so must the Son of man be lifted up: That whosoever believeth in him should not perish, but have everlasting life*—the solar force, the Christ force, the Christ life and light. I come into you that you may use this creative force, become a being of light having dominion over the earth and over all creatures of the earth. I come that you may become master of your life, of your body, of your conditions, of your circumstances in the world. *I am the way, the truth and the life.*

We cannot find language which will clothe the beauty, the glory of that solar body. The 'plumed serpents' are those who have passed along the same pathway as you journey, and who are portrayed as wearing wings with a radiance around their head. The serpent fire, which is rising, having taken full possession, the head becomes radiant with plumes of the inner light, the light of the sun shining from it.*

Soul-development, Past and Present

Remember that the sole purpose of your life is to grow first of all in self-consciousness—that is, consciousness of yourself as an individual. Then you expand your consciousness to take in those around you, those with whom you live. Shall we call this a family consciousness, a group consciousness, or better still a consciousness of the whole brotherhood of life? You have sometimes felt in meditation the intense joy that comes with this realization of spiritual brotherhood (which of course is the true spiritual communion), or with the development of the soul towards awareness and the needs of those around it. In the same degree as the individuals progress, so the whole race approaches this point of broth-

*The term 'the plumed serpent' is well discussed in Grace Cooke's book THE ILLUMINED ONES (White Eagle Publishing Trust, 1966)

erhood and awareness. You may feel that many centuries may elapse before the world can respond. Nevertheless, we assure you that during the coming fifty years, you will be astonished at the soul-progress of the world, because within this time unbelievable changes will come.

Instead of perpetual war, brotherhood between all things and all people will be established. Today such a statement seems incredible. Nevertheless, the next stage is already developing: that state in which men and women become aware of their true relationship to their brethren. Then will come an expansion still further, towards God-consciousness or cosmic consciousness. Beyond that is the consciousness of the Solar Logos, the solar consciousness. This is taking you a long way ahead. However, read our words and meditate upon this truth, because a truth so beautiful and wonderful can be both a help and inspiration. This vision of the future life will make you feel that your present striving is very, very well worth the effort. Remember: if you are listening to the voice of the spirit, you are pioneers working for the great day when cosmic and solar consciousness will be the gift or the realization of all peoples.

Know that the world is not going to remain in its present state of chaos. We cannot find words suitable to convey a deeper and indeed infinite truth, because it would be like trying to teach a kindergarten school a lesson in higher mathematics. You see, you cannot possibly absorb or understand deeper spiritual truths until you are able to comprehend some of the infinite possibilities both within and before you. This, you will see, is the same law as operates when you first open the door of your consciousness to spirit communication. Everything depends upon the soul which is seeking that communication. All depends upon your own level of spiritual growth and upon your understanding of occult and spiritual law. So it must be, from the beginning in the kindergarten. In a higher class you are able to comprehend more advanced lessons, but everything depends upon you. There is truth. There is glory. *I AM the way, the truth and the life*, the Christ said. That life is within you, but until you have unfolded and until you have gained mastery over yourself, you cannot possibly comprehend the greater mysteries.

You are apt to talk too glibly about the Son of God and the Christ. You accept the Christ as an ideal, and some of you rightly recognize the Christ spirit as gentle and meek and loving, something that is wholly at-one with something within yourself. You fail, though, to understand the immense glory of that great Solar Logos, which is the life of all human beings, and which is also the life of this planet. Neither do you understand, dear ones, that this outpouring of golden light comes down and reaches you—if you are sufficiently humble and simple and can open your heart to this blessing. It is like a spark which bursts into fire. Remember that you hold within yourself that solar force, in a much smaller degree. It is within you, buried deeply, and lies there sleeping. This is better so, until you rise of your own freewill to worship truth, to worship and adore the Son of God, not in some egotistical way but profoundly from the depths of your being.

When once the soul feels adoration and worship for the Solar Logos, the blazing Sun in the heaven—which is in other words the only-begotten Son of the Father–Mother God—that soul feels a stirring within, just as the mother feels the quickening of her babe under her heart. It is exactly the same. Now will come the rising of this solar force into your etheric body, into your physical body, into all your bodies and into every centre. These centres will begin to pulsate and will open as a flower opens to the sunlight. From here, you will progress from realization of your brotherhood with your companions to the realization of your at-one-ment with the Christ. You will be overshadowed and impressed with this new-breaking consciousness of God.

You will be able to recognize yourself as a true yogi. Do not think that the term means someone who walks around with a begging bowl. A yogi is one who has attained union with God-consciousness.

Many men and women now living can be truly called yogis. This is for you also. You can attain to this degree of God-consciousness, of union with God. From this stage, you can go forth into solar consciousness, which is a condition beyond your comprehension, but something that waits for you in the future.

Perfected Being

Down the ages the temples and the mystery schools were formed for the special purpose of giving sincere and earnest enquirers an opportunity to become pupils. They helped truly simple and earnest souls enquiring into the mysteries of life and the soul, and those of the life after death and onward. It was never easy to get into a mystery school. They taught both the lesser and the greater mysteries of life. To receive such knowledge the soul of the student must be pure and simple, because otherwise the unfolding or passing-on of knowledge of the mysteries might prove dangerous.

This, as we have said, actually happened in ages past. As a result, the whole equilibrium of the earth planet became disturbed and upset. The results are very dire when these spiritual forces are misused by one who is instructed in them. For this reason the training of the soul can prove severe, particularly if the soul will not accept in simple faith and trust the order or the plan that is laid out for it.

In the mystery school the student was taught how to uncover this solar fire, this solar force, and use it for the glorification of God and for the blessing and upliftment of its fellow creatures. This was to be done not only living the life of a saint but also by doing the works of the Father–Mother in heaven. We can assure you, brethren, that this spirit of Christ is coming into the hearts of millions. The coming of the Lord is nigh!

This sounds somewhat evangelistic. It is true, though, for the light of Christ will stimulate in every woman and man the spirit of the solar fire, the Christ spirit. Of their own freewill they will throw away personal weapons. They will, in the words of the bible, *beat their swords into ploughshares*. They will throw away the weapons of war. They will meet their brothers and sisters and greet them as in the old days of the mystery school, when one gripped the hand of another in perfect comradeship and love. This is the second coming; and the church of the new age will be this church of the Light of God, the church of the Sun brothers and sisters, the church of the living, loving Christ.

VIII

THERE ARE NO SHORT CUTS!

He that believeth on me, the works that I do shall he do also, and greater works than these shall he do.

John 14 : 12

YOU FIND LIFE difficult sometimes, and feel despairing about the world, and more especially about yourselves. We of the Great Brotherhood in spirit bring you power and love and wisdom to help you. We know there is great eagerness in the hearts of some of you to get on with the work. You want to do something to help the work of the Great Brotherhood for the spiritual upliftment and evolution of human kind, and you are tempted to seek ways and means of development and service. There are some of you who may have thought that this development can be hurried.

In one way this is possible, for it is in the plan of the Infinite Wisdom that there shall be at this time a special outpouring of the Light upon humanity, so that humanity can speed up its own spiritual evolution. There is, however, one truth which we should like to make very clear, and this is that there are no short cuts. There is a difference between speeding up evolution and taking a short cut to heaven. The first of these is possible—indeed, it is now presented to human kind—but the second is entirely outside the plan. You cannot take a short cut in life.

Every lesson has to be thoroughly absorbed and put into practice. However, with the baptism of light which all the heavens are pouring upon the earth now, those souls who have earned this special opportunity towards rapid initiation into the heavenly life will be able to make a big stride forward. You will notice this in the world. You have already noticed the many groups that are being formed, and the opportunity which has been given to the masses, and will be given with increasing power, to learn about the spiritual powers within. At the moment, though, human kind is going through rather a dangerous stage on the path. Hitherto these secrets have been kept from the bulk of humanity. Only for those who entered the Mystery Schools has there been the opportunity to qualify for this knowledge. Now in this new age of Aquarius, the gate of initiation is being opened wide; and herein lies the danger. Humanity has to discriminate and discern. Many will join groups to learn how to unfold the light which is within; and the true power to heal the sick, and to reach out to the soul of a brother or a sister, lies in this unfoldment.

The light which is generated by any of you during the course of your spiritual unfoldment is a very real and tangible thing. It radiates from every pupil who unfolds their inner gifts, and it really penetrates the soul of another. It is a very sacred power to be used with delicacy and discernment.

Right now, your intuition is awakening and urging you to seek, seek, seek for the light. So great is this desire that you go hither and thither in your search, and quite frequently complete confusion is the result. You encounter so many contradictions in your search. The mind is greedy. You delight to hear about your own incarnations, long to have greater knowledge of your own life in this past. This is all symptomatic. When you are really ready to look into the mirror of your own soul, you will see just how agreeable—or the reverse—has been your past; and it takes a strong and wise soul to be able to face the truth.

The difficult part is for a soul to live, day by day, in a dark world, absorbing the lessons which the outer life is intended to teach. Above all, we would ask you to cast out all fear. If you persevere with this one small lesson for even just a few weeks, at the end of that time you will realize what a great step forward you have taken. Be without fear. Surrender to God. You will be filled with love and light; you will help the world forward towards peace and will help all those who are in darkness because they are full of fear—even your so-called enemies.

There are no short cuts to the Promised Land. You may get a ladder (and we will call this ladder the intellect) and run up it and peep over the wall into the Promised Land and see it flowing with milk and honey.* There are many people who thus climb and look over and think they know; they think they have reached the Promised Land. But it is only an illusion. There is but one way to arrive at the Promised Land, and that is by becoming suitably clothed in the right raiment, a raiment made out of the very substance of the Promised Land. This means that the soul can only know the Promised Land by becoming an inhabitant of it, by living patiently and happily and never losing sight of the guiding light from above, never allowing the light to go out in the heart.

One last thing. When you have learned to hear the voice of intuition, your reason will not take primary place. Reason will have served its purpose in your life, and its domination will pass away, like all other things do when their purpose has been fulfilled. Out of reason will come intuition, or the divine intelligence of the God self. But unless you give intuition an opportunity to grow and develop in your soul, you will respond for a long time to the harsh note of reason, and be bound in its chains.

The Essential Lesson

May it inspire you with a clearer vision and a deeper peace, as you realize that life is governed by perfect justice. The law must forever operate to bring men and women to face themselves.

Humanity actually spends its time running away from itself, seeking dissipation and oblivion; which is no more than frittering away

* Joshua 5 : 6

the happiness and joy which God would give. Witness the many distractions you have created for yourselves in your life today, amusements which compel people's attention. Do not think, for one moment, that we do not recognize the need for recreation; but learn to take your relaxation and recreation in the true and harmonious spirit. Do not dissipate the energies of the spirit, or the life-force within your body, which is the temple of the Most High.... The essential lesson, we repeat, that life has to teach humanity is to face itself.

We urge all pupils to strive particularly for discrimination in selecting their path, because there will arise teachers who have a certain amount of knowledge, and will give forth a great deal of matter. There will be some who will be swept off their course by this outpouring of words. Always remember that although words have their place, and are useful to open the door, you cannot advance into the Temple of Initiation on words alone! The passwords on the spiritual plane are not spoken words only. Passwords are sounded in the heart, and you cannot advance into the Temple of Initiation without sounding the password of the heart centre. It is one thing to read and to listen to words and to have all knowledge, but you cannot have the power of Christ without the password, which is love ... love. In other words, you cannot have the power without being love.

All the great social problems you face, from war to the greed you see in society, are due to breaking the law of love. It is largely by suffering that humanity learns to listen to the elder brethren, who, from time to time, restate the simple truth. This truth, this path, consists of ways of service to relieve suffering, to help the younger brethren towards harmony and happiness, towards Christ, the ultimate goal of every soul! The path is very difficult to find; and being found, very difficult to walk steadfastly, because there is so much to cloud the vision. The only way to maintain a foothold and to progress is not by taking up this or that path, but by entering the chamber within: by praying, with all one's strength, to the wisdom of God. When light comes, it will be not the light of intellect alone, but a light which urges the soul to love all.

The Christ Light

All seek the light, yet not before others is your light lit: not even disclosed to your nearest and dearest, but in the innermost sanctuary, with no veil between you and your real self. When with all your power you call upon God to be alight in your heart, then in that instant, the light shines forth. As you uncover the light, you unconsciously aspire to the heaven world, to the home of Christ, to the realm of divine spirit. Nothing intervenes, for the light placed within you is the Christ light. The light waxes bright and sends forth a radiance which encircles you; for the little pinpoint of light is that ancient symbol—the centre of the circle from which no true brother or sister can err. And as the circle round you is completed, so God sends forth power to reinforce the light from the Son—you.

This is the secret of the white magic. No harm can break through when the Christ is manifesting through you. The time is drawing near for the Christ, the Grand Master, to come again among people. Do you realize that channels are needed, vehicles which are pure—such as that prepared by Jesus of Nazareth? Pure physical bodies, pure astral or desire bodies, and pure mental bodies are needed, so that the divine light, the light of Christ, may come again and use such channels to help humanity—no, more than help, to save humanity. For the time approaches when those souls not ready to respond to the spiritual force about to descend upon earth will fall back, recede, and wait until the next great life-urge comes forth.

When you pray and meditate to help your brethren on earth, do not think only of peace; give forth the Christ light. Light ... light; the light which holds the balance: this is what works the magic.

Now must come forth into physical manifestation that flower of perfect being, the son–daughter of God, the Christ man–woman; not only through the one Jesus but through all—through all who can respond sufficiently. This is the second coming of Christ. As you become illumined with the Christ within, your vision will be opened, and you will see the one who is the Master, the Perfect One. Yes, you will see him–her in the perfect glory of the human form. As Jesus healed with his touch, or by his thought to the suffering at a distance, so too may you heal at a touch and by thought. *He that believeth on me, the works that I do shall he do also, and greater works than these shall he do.*

Hope

At spring time the word 'hope' echoes across the countryside, and you hope for better days, looking forward with a faith that your earth will be crowned with blossoms and sun and beauty. This is our message to you all: *hope.* If only you could check yourselves, and stop being sorrowful and grumbling! We know that you have sorrows; that you witness the sufferings of others. We who see a little deeper recognize a strange beauty beneath the sufferings of humanity. Behind every experience, every sorrow, every saddening, sordid thing there is reason, a great purpose. Some day, somewhere, somehow you will know that there is no difference between intense sorrow and intense joy. A mystery of the spirit? Yes: you cannot understand these things now, but when you have learned the lesson, understanding will come.

We give you hope. You are marching forward; the earth plane, the earth planet as a whole, moves forward with its whole being towards becoming itself like a sun. Earth's humanity has awakened, and slowly, almost imperceptibly, humanity responds and raises itself, even as a child stirs in the womb. The earth is surely moving towards its own birth: it will become spiritualized, so that its very crust, its outer substance, is changed and transcended.

In the same way, human life moves towards such a birth. It moves into glory, into freedom. Every experience brings to humanity growth towards spiritual consciousness. Nothing is wasted in life: no experience whatsoever. However hard the lessons have been for you, and maybe at this moment are, may it comfort and inspire you to be told that they are worthwhile. Humanity makes progress: it does not regress, and every method used to bring about its birth into the spiritual life is necessary. Look out upon the world as it is with tolerance and love and hope. There is no death! Progress, progress, progress ... growth; a life-force ever moving onward, forward into the Sun. Hope!

IX

THE WHITE EAGLE

I John, who also am your brother, and companion in tribulation, and in the kingdom and patience of Jesus Christ, was in the isle that is called Patmos, for the word of God.

Revelation 1 : 9

[Despite the bustle of modern tourist life, the Greek island of Patmos is still a quiet place. High above the main town, amongst eucalyptus and pine trees, the white-domed sanctuary building sits above the natural rock cave where St John the Divine was visited by the angel, and was thus inspired to record the book Revelation. There is a time-less quality about the whole setting, and something significant about the long, arduous climb, up steep steps, to reach it. First the climb up, and then the shorter series of steps down under the building to the cave—an upward and an inner movement to reach the place of stillness and receptivity. The cool interior is welcoming after the heat of the Greek sun, and there is a poignancy about seeing the rock pillow, with its shallow depression in the centre, where St John is reputed to have rested his head, when the angel came to him and lent him vision.

A.P.H.]

*He that overcometh shall inherit all things: and I will be his God,
and he shall be my son.*

Revelation 21 : 7

If I will that he tarry till I come, what is that to thee?

John 21 : 22

*And I John saw the holy city, new Jerusalem, coming down from God
out of heaven, prepared as a bride adorned for her husband....*

*And he shewed me a pure river of water of life, clear as crystal,
proceeding out of the throne of God and of the Lamb,*

*In the midst of the street of it, and on either side of the river, was
there the tree of life, which bare twelve manner of fruits, and yielded
the fruit every month: and the leaves of the tree were for the healing
of the nations.*

Revelation 21 : 1–2; 22 : 1–2

In my father's house are many mansions.

John 14 : 2

THE SECRET OF the individual John is not known to many on earth.
By exercise of intellect alone, you will always fail to read the eternal
truths. We have outlined already the mystical interpretation of the mis-
sion of he who was known as John. An earnest study of the message of
John reveals to those with understanding that the things he taught concerned the power of the soul. The Gospels of Matthew, Luke and Mark
are accounts of a unique man and his words and acts; that of John is
concerned with this person's inner being. Jesus' coming actually heralded the Aquarian Age, the age when human kind will arise in spiritual light; when men and women will learn to use the full power of the
soul, by reason of knowledge concerning each and all the vehicles comprising that temple which is the human being.

The Revelation of St John contains an outline of universal evolution
from the beginning to the end. We do not wish to be too explicit, to say:
'Lo, here is fact; lo, there is fact!'. Rather, you must respond to the light

in your heart, and see the vision glorious for yourselves. John is he who is yet to come—yes, in fuller manifestation—to the children of earth. He came in lesser degree with the one known as his beloved and to all people as Jesus of Nazareth ... but will return, this time in all his glory.

Some speculate about the death of John: where did he die? Where was his body buried? John never died! Did not Jesus Christ say, *If I will that he tarry till I come, what is that to thee?* With these words he showed his acceptance of John's being more than just a human being: but rather, representative of the human soul, tarrying on earth until the divine life ... light ... word ... Son, comes again to gather its beloved. Only those souls who cannot respond must then be left sleeping in the darkness, until once again the light comes—long, long after.

The Symbols of the New Age

We have said to you that as the Aquarian Age advances there will come a stimulation and development of the occult power in humanity. You have also heard us say that the development of occult power can be dangerous. Without the Christ light growing and developing in your being, you cannot with safety advance into this next stage of development, which is the unfoldment of the occult powers which each of you has within you. This is the reason why Jesus, the Christ, came to prepare people's minds and souls for the next age.

The master Jesus is also the master at the head of the sixth ray, that of the higher mind, of philosophy and healing, and of the philosophy of love. We see the Piscean Age, the age of the soul and the emotions, as a preparation for the next step, which is the age of the spirit—the Aquarian Age. During this cycle the new church will be born—the church of St John—and there will be revealed to humanity the esoteric, or the inner meaning of the spiritual life. Humanity will learn that men and women do not live by bread alone, but draw sustenance from the universal, spiritual life; and that they do this through the seven gateways, or the seven windows in the soul.

In the early Christian era the church of St Peter was established:

which church, we are told, was built upon a rock—the rock being the mental disposition of the people. That the church is built upon a rock means that there are worshippers and even preachers who remain bound to the materialistic doctrine. Some even go so far as to say they do not know if there is an afterlife. They will provide you with an ethical teaching, but as to spiritual realization and the coming into the many mansions spoken of by the master Jesus, they say nothing.

By contrast, in the new age that is upon us the psychic and spiritual forces within each human being will be stimulated. You will learn how to open the windows of your soul, how to open the chakras and go forth like a winged being into the heavenly spheres. A spiritual unfoldment of your inner faculties will take place and human consciousness will progress to great heights.

As the Piscean Age had as its symbol the fishes, so the Aquarian Age has the symbol of the white eagle. The white eagle is the symbol of the great mystic St John. The eagle is also the higher aspect of Scorpio, and in this we see symbolised the arising in humanity of the power and the wisdom of kundalini, or the arising of the divine fire. In the centre of kundalini are cradled the divine fires of life, the creative powers. These creative powers can find expression in animal instincts, but remember that they are seats of the God in everyone; they contain the powers of creation and the powers of aspiration, consummation, transmutation. As each person slowly evolves from animal to god—the human being made perfect—these fires are what raise him or her aloft to heaven as on the eagle's wings. All that was centred in the lower instincts is evolving, rising higher in the person's consciousness, until he or she becomes illumined. This is the esoteric interpretation of the truth which the symbol of the white eagle represents.

In the new age, the power of kundalini will be stimulated by influences from the heavens. Messengers—you may call them angels because an angel is a messenger from the heavens—will be coming, bringing a ray of light and knowledge which will teach humanity how to rise, how to develop its wings. As a symbol of the new age, the white eagle soars into the heavens and sees far and wide.

You have been given another symbol for the age of Aquarius, which is that of the figure carrying the water pot. The figure pours forth the waters of the spirit, the living waters, upon the earth. You remember the master Jesus telling his disciples to follow the man carrying the water pot, who would lead them to an inn and there take them to an upper room—the interpretation of which is the man or woman's higher state of consciousness. The head centre is the upper room, the upper chamber.

There they were to make ready for the coming of their master. In the same way, the higher mind is to be made ready for the incoming of the Christ spirit, or illumination by the divine. The Sun is the divine fire within the soul of every son and daughter of God. So the higher mind has to be prepared before the Christ can enter in. You see the symbolism of this? Each son and daughter has first to train him or herself in pure thought, pure living. Then this person has to aspire to higher and better forms of worship, higher and better forms of life. In doing this, the person makes ready for the incoming of divine illumination.

In some traditions the symbol of the Aquarian Age is an angelic figure, that of the complete, the perfected man–woman. Again, this means that there will come the transmutation of the creative forces in the human from the lower to the higher centre. In the Revelation of St John will be found set forth the mysteries of the evolution of the spirit and the creative powers within the human body which have to be transmuted from the 'animal' instincts to the mental and spiritual plane.

At the commencement of the Aquarian Age there is a period of great outpouring of spirit upon the people. You will find in every quarter that the most unexpected men and women will be demonstrating to the world that they are the instruments of the spirit. Look for the secret key, look for the figure carrying the water pot, look for the person in your everyday life who is being quickened in spirit. Do not be foolish in your looking, be very still and wise: but we reiterate, keep on the lookout for the quickening of the spirit in earthly people, and especially in so-called worldly people; because often the worldly people are the people of experience and great humanity. They know and understand the temptations and the pains and the suffering of human life. These are the people who will be displaying the power of the spirit. Look for the man of spirit, he who carries the water pot, the Aquarian.

The Book of Revelation

John, our beloved brother, has shed upon the soul of humanity a deep mystical revelation. Scholars have endeavoured to interpret his meaning but, with few exceptions, only the husk has been garnered, the true grain neglected. The teachings contained in the Gospel, in the Epistles of St John, and in the Revelation of John, have been attributed to many sources. By some it has been said that the Revelation is merely a restatement of the Greek and Egyptian mysteries, which mysteries were introduced into Christianity.

The Revelation of John is truly a portrayal of the ancient wisdom, its truths concealed under a wealth of symbolism, majestic and wonderful, even if they are sometimes violent and full of dire warning. *As it was in the beginning, is now, and ever shall be: world without end!* As then, so today: if you would understand your own creation, your own evolution, the life to which you go, the purpose you must follow, you must seek deeply within your own breast where truth abides; and so realize the spiritual life—the life invisible—which interpenetrates every form of matter ... and find this life invisible to be the living word of God.

There are said to be seven different interpretations of St John's Revelation, and even that would be limiting the number. The vision of John enshrines the mystery of the whole universe, from the beginning to the end—not only of the creation of the world and the solar system of this earth, but also the human lifespan: the mysteries of the microcosm and of the macrocosm. Many of the references to beasts and animals and to the fiery signs refer also to astronomical or astrological truths. Although certain constellations are referred to, remember we are dealing mainly with the evolution of the human soul. Nevertheless, with the continual reincarnations which the soul undergoes, there must, sooner or later, be brought to bear upon the soul the influences of each sign of the zodiac.

Revelation clearly indicates the Fall of humanity. It charts humanity's long descent through the seven spheres, from its original purity and pristine innocence. It charts the watchful guardianship of the angels; the clothing of the human soul and spirit with ever denser conditions, vehicles or bodies: ever more binding limitation with ever more stringent stress and struggle. It shows how at last, after many, many life-episodes or incarnations, the soul (enriched greatly by experience) turns again Godward.

Many feel that the prophecies in Revelation refer to actual physical happenings. This is also true, though not perhaps as you would think. For as the lifestreams* are sent forth, each produces a root race. The cycles of life move not so much in circular as in spiral form. The spiral of existence ever traces and retraces a circle; and yet with each round, existence becomes raised. With each cycle, the collective human soul moves to a higher vibration, nearer to heaven. At the end of each vast round the cosmic forces, the two great powers—good and evil—become so active in operation that there comes an explosion.

Such upheavals can be seen throughout the ages. The story of the flood in the Christian bible refers to the sinking of Atlantis, where the two forces actually disturbed the equilibrium of the cosmos, and caused the destruction of the life of that continent—a great purification. Understand that the Armageddon you read of in Revelation does not mean some frightful struggle between nations, but the individual encounters which each soul must attempt ... the progress or evolution of the microcosm, that which will come to each soul: upheaval, cleansing, purification. At certain periods in the world's history this must take place. But as below, so above; and when we refer to Armageddon as being foreshadowed on the higher, or spiritual planes, this is in accordance with John. He is dealing, almost exclusively, with the progress or evolution of the microcosm. There must come to every soul that upheaval, cleansing, purification; the war between the higher and the lower in the self must be fought out. This comes, not necessarily in cataclysmic form as in the past. There can, of course, be war on the inner planes, war on the astral, which of course has its repercussion on the earth. But we stress

*For a full account by White Eagle of what he means by 'the lifestreams', see WALKING WITH THE ANGELS (White Eagle Publishing Trust, 1998)

the point that St John refers definitely to the war between the higher and the lower self.

There is one definite purpose in life and that is progress; what appears to be retrogression is only a form of ultimate progress. But you must not lose sight of the fact that humanity is progressing on the spiral; the experience of yesterday may be the experience of tomorrow, but on a higher vibration.

The Golden City

We should like you to grow in your consciousness of that Golden City referred to in the words of St John.

Where is this City to be found? Is it something external? Or is it something within you yourselves? It is both, my friends. First of all, it is deep within you all. Yet what is within has eventually to become externalised, or expressed outside you. Do you know that when a soul passes away after death, the condition in which it finds itself reflects the thoughts and feelings with which it habitually lived while in the physical body? Its surroundings are those of its own thought, its own aspirations, externalised. With whatever a person fills his or her thoughts on earth, he or she will, to begin with, surround him or herself in the life beyond. Even your homes will be externalised—libraries, much-loved pictures, beloved gardens, favourite places of holiday—all that has delighted the soul will be exactly what it will find when it lives in the world of spirit.

A man or woman grows spiritually, just as a child grows to adulthood, and afterwards continues to grow from the human estate to the angelic estate. There is a passage in the bible which says that the human being, if he–she 'overcometh' all things, shall become God's son— and angel.* There are planes of life undreamt-of by you, you who are imprisoned in earthiness. But this does not mean that comprehension of these glories in the heavens cannot be realized while you are living in the physical body.

*Revelation is full of promises of the rewards which will come to those who overcome all things. For one such promise, see the headnotes to this chapter.

When a soul grows in awareness of God through aspiration, meditation, prayer and love, that soul is being prepared for initiation into the Golden City. You read that this City has twelve foundations—the twelve foundations being the twelve qualities of the soul, the essential qualities upon which to build 'Jerusalem' within the soul. The twelve gates referred to, and the twelve tribes, we interpret as meaning the twelve perfected types of men and women, the twelve perfect signs of the zodiac. Three gates each were at the North, the South, the East, and West. Are these not Earth, Air, Fire and Water, the elements with which each soul builds the perfect City?

There is another important realization. John says there is no sea in the new heaven and the new earth.* We offer you the thought that this means that there is no division, no dividing line between earth and heaven; that in this new City, this new state of life to which everyone is advancing, there will be an interpenetration of all life, both heavenly and earthly. We see in this the perfect balance expressed by the symbol of the six-pointed Star. All seers know that heaven and earth interpenetrate, and this must be manifested in human form. When the seer sees a vision, when in the higher faculties the seer walks in the golden streets of the Golden City, he or she knows that it does not incapacitate him or her for daily work, but gives a more perfect body and mind, a more perfect spiritual life, lived both on earth and in heaven.

The division which the sea symbolises has eventually to be done away with. It will be overcome and there will be a perfect interpenetration of the heavenly and the earth life. This heavenly city is paralleled by the Chinese teaching about the Golden Flower. The Golden City and the Golden Flower stand for the centre of the heart, that innermost state which all can reach. It is the state of divine illumination, which comes to all through aspiration and true meditation. The New Jerusalem is built upon the foundation of the twelve virtues of life. When you read that the angel takes the measuring rod of a hundred and forty-four cubits, and finds the perfect cube, the perfect square,* this means that

*The architecture of the holy city, and the absence of any sea, are described in Revelation 21

the human soul perfected is represented by the perfect square: and the number of the perfect human is nine; represented by the digits of the number 144 added together.*

You yourself are the temple within the city of God; you are yourself the perfect cube perfected through experience and perhaps through suffering, but at all events through your human relationships. Through life after life all your excrescences are smoothed away until you become the perfect lodge or temple for the indwelling Christ. When you become a transparent channel through which the divine light of the Father–Mother God flows, then you become the perfect healer of individuals; and individuals, remember, make up a nation, and nations a world.

Do you recognize the vital importance of each person realizing the purpose for which he or she was created, realizing his or her true son–daughtership with God, so that he or she may be a healer of the nations? At this time in the world's history such healing is most vital. How can there be reconstruction of cities, reforming of nations, until the clear, crystal river of life, light and healing mentioned by John washes clean the world?

The New Jerusalem is the soul made perfect, man–woman made perfect. This, my friends, is the goal of all seekers after truth. Do not think, either, that it is just a condition which awaits you thousands upon thousands of years hence. You can begin to understand this perfect life now. When a soul becomes attuned to the perfect life (which is love and wisdom and power), it becomes the clear and perfect cube of light, and through it flows a crystal river which comes from the very heart of the Cosmos.

John saw *a new heaven and a new earth*—the holy city—like to a new and more perfect Jerusalem. There is no further need for earthly sun or moon. God, the spirit, is the spiritual sun; the soul, the spiritual moon; and the street of the city is of gold, clear as glass. The initiate walks always the golden path, and has neither dross, nor shadow.

Would that we had words to describe the Golden City! But you can

*Revelation 21 : 17

yourselves win through to understanding. Indeed, you cannot fail, although you may postpone and delay. As you walk the path of life steadfastly, with watchfulness and prayer—slowly, patiently labouring to subdue the lower nature, to overcome those turbulent emotions which would override the better self—be assured that by daily effort, daily striving for poise and mastery and balance, then step by step the vehicles of the higher life become purified, until they are able to respond to the heavenly influences.

Is this not a vision worth striving after, worth living for? We assure you that all the confusion, all the sickness of body and mind, all the inconvenience and the sorrows and the separation of this present time on earth, all fall away when this true vision is established in the heart, in the mind, in the soul of a man or woman. Beloved brethren, when Jesus wept over Jerusalem, he wept not just over the city in Palestine, but for the suffering and sorrowful soul of man–woman.*

We leave you with thanksgiving to our Creator. May divine peace enfold you all; may divine truth be uncovered, deep though it may lie, within your consciousness. May you see this vision of the New Jerusalem that lies within your innermost being; and then may your vision be externalised on earth, on all the planes of life.

*Luke 19 : 41

X

THE AGE OF INTUITION

The way to truth is through the spirit. In the outer world there is turmoil and chaos and unhappiness. You think with the mortal mind, with the mind which is part of the substance of earth. You should think with your inner mind, you should approach problems through the inner self, through intuition. The very word explains itself. In-tuition—training inside yourself. You are looking outside for help, and all the time the help you want is inside. The world of spirit that so many of you talk about and believe in, and long to touch, is all within.

White Eagle, THE QUIET MIND

THE PISCEAN AGE has been an age of the soul and emotions. Christianity, for instance, is a religion where the emotions are stirred, made use of, in its devotions. The emotional body is indeed a vehicle through which the higher influences of heaven can reach humanity. But in the Aquarian Age it will be through the higher spiritual body, the intuitional body, that they will come. Through the intuition a new creative spirit will come to humanity.

In this new age a new religion is being established, which will not deal in words only. It will not only preach the gospel—it will interpret for its followers the mystic signs and symbols of the age. It will teach the people how to unfold their own Godlike powers, so that they may use the spiritual forces for the blessing of human kind. It is not knowledge alone that humanity needs, but development of an inner power which is sometimes called, in its early stages, intuition. Intuition can evolve to such a degree it becomes knowledge, absolute and certain knowledge of the God-life. This power flows through the hands, through the eyes, through the aura of people who have unfolded it. Such brethren walk the world carrying with them healing power. They are the peacemakers. This is the ability to reach and enter that higher plane of consciousness at any time, in any condition of life.

Psychic phenomena will become of greater moment to many people in the new age. The ancient wisdom is stirring in the hearts of many. Some of you have already received certain training in opening up the sacred centres of power within your own being. With the advance of spiritual growth in the race, already a sixth sense is developing. In the near future, scientists will discover, or are already discovering, that life and even physical matter has a spiritual origin. It will be proven that life is not material (as it appears) but is in reality a state of consciousness which is fluid, spiritual. In the mystery schools of the past, the pupils were taught how to unfold these inner powers, but the knowledge was not given to all because of the danger that those powers might be misused either ignorantly or with knowledge and selfishly. We want to make absolutely clear the dangers and the blessings of unfolding the inner powers and tapping into the spheres of consciousness beyond the normal mind. Candidates in the ancient mystery schools had to pass severe tests of their integrity, purity and loyalty before they were admitted.

It is not wise to force the development of the psychic centres, but it is in the plan of evolution that these centres must be vivified, and in full operation, before the man–woman is complete. At the present time human kind—or many members of the human race—have reached a point where the vitalizing of the centres is desirable.

Developing the Mind in the Heart

The great white light of Christ is the healer of all ills of body and of soul. It heals the physical body, and is the great solvent of all shadows. It is ever the builder, ever the constructor, and you are called by the hosts invisible into service with the light, into action.

'How'—we hear your unspoken question—'How can we serve, how should we act?' You must endeavour to become aware of the invisible forces which are playing upon the earth life. You must train your body and your higher vehicles to become consciously aware of this stream of light which finds entrance into your being through the psychic centres; you must learn to be aware of this circulating light stream which vivifies and can glorify body and soul, and pass from you, directed by your highest self, to heal the sick throughout the world—the sick in body and mind. The vibrations and the power of the angels and the great spiritual beings work through human channels to build heaven into the human consciousness. This is the temple training of the past, according to the ancient wisdom: becoming aware of the land of light, becoming aware of the light within the soul; of the effect of colour upon the soul, upon the mind, upon the body ... the effect of perfume ... the effect of sound.

The time has now come for you all to develop your sixth sense, which we call intuition. Humanity has for long concentrated upon the stimulation and development of intellect. This sixth sense, or ray of light, is destined to open for you the secrets of nature, of creation, and all spiritual life and purpose. We ourselves work especially on this ray of intuition, the love-wisdom ray. And so when you and we and the company of spiritual brethren meet together in the inner sanctuary, we meet in love, desiring one of the most precious gifts of life—wisdom, through love.

The unfoldment of the psychic or spiritual centres can be quickened by love in the heart, but development of love without knowledge is not enough. If you are only sending out love, you can get into a complacent, dreamy state; but with the opening of the higher centres you can work with knowledge. Knowledge should be coupled with love, love with wisdom; it is necessary to develop the wisdom aspect. We know that all things can be done with love; but if you do not get knowledge, love can be compared to the flower which has not opened. Strive for knowledge; strive for full consciousness and understanding of what you are doing in the higher planes.

In your meditation, you are being taught how to bring the higher chakras to life: that is, how to open your consciousness to the pure, the spiritual level of life. This is the right way to unfold the inner faculties. The sixth sense, the intuition, functions from the heart centre. In meditation, in true contemplation of the Deity and all that is holy, you are opening up that centre. The safe way and the correct way for spiritual unfoldment is to work from the heart of love. The soul-consciousness is situated in the brain. The divine spirit, we suggest, dwells in the heart. You are opening the throat centre, too, for pure speech and knowledge— knowledge which comes from the fifth sphere, the sphere of Mercury. With the development of the throat centre comes inspiration for speech.

The One who is the light, the Christ within, lives in the heart centre. The physical organ—the heart—bears a sacred relationship to the spiritual centre in the etheric body situated over the heart. When death takes place, the divine spark, the seed-atom of the spirit, is withdrawn from the heart. When this is understood, it can be readily accepted that the life of the spirit functions through the heart centre. It is called love. Your heart, then, is the centre of intuition.

As we speak to you, one great truth which occurs to you is the need to contact, not only mentally but spiritually, the eternal truths of life— a contact made with the mind of the heart. Many schools find the intellectual way is their path; it is so because the intellect has need to grow and expand. But there are those in incarnation who do not need to pass along the intellectual path in order to gain or absorb the eternal truths. Many find the way of the heart easier, and certainly we work on the love-wisdom ray. So we would reveal, not in words alone, but in essence, the glorious light of the spirit.

There are many ways of learning the inner mysteries, not necessarily through written or spoken words. If the soul can attune itself to higher planes of love and wisdom, the mind in the heart will absorb; and although the outer mind does not always immediately interpret the truth thus absorbed, nevertheless later the mind will begin to interpret and in time know great truths, for the heart does not register incorrectly. That which the heart absorbs is truth. In this present age this sense of intuition is developing; through the intuition, hitherto insoluble truths will be solved—truths insoluble to the materialist, however great the intellect. The mind of the heart will know, will understand, these greater mysteries.

One example of this is how the memory of previous incarnations can be recalled, as the soul strives to reach the higher consciousness, outside the limitations of the physical brain. With many people, it is just a nebulous feeling. Or it may be that the soul is aware of certain tastes and characteristics brought back from the past—love of embroidery from China, love of dancing from Greece or Spain, love of Egyptian art. Some little trait in the character may betray a link with some past civilization. These memories do not come through the earthly brain, so much as through the spiritual brain, centred in the heart. It is through the mind in the heart that contact with eternity is made. It is almost another name for intuition.

So the intuition has to be developed. Mistakes do not matter. In comparison with the greater and wiser ones, we all make mistakes. Certainly it is right to strive to develop the intuition, but make sure that the inner voice comes from the heart of wisdom, and not from the self that wants something, the desire self. Intuition comes like a flash, it is an inward knowing. The thing is to have courage to act on it; to be prepared for whatever it brings. The intuition can be developed in meditation, not through activity of the mind, but through quiet contemplation within the sanctuary of the heart.

Emotional Control

Let us consider the inner world of which we speak. To you it will appear a mental world, because when you withdraw from the outer, the physical life, you seem to go inward. Then it appears you are living in your mind. However, this inner world is not only a world of thought, but also a world of feeling. You are getting beneath thought, and thus you come to a world of finer feeling, or an emotional world. Although they may not realize it, all people live in such a world of emotion, yet this emotional life is also affected by the mental world around them, or by the thoughts of others. It therefore becomes part of your training or development of spiritual insight, of clairvoyance and illumination, for you to learn to protect your fine emotional body from the harsh thoughts of the outer world. For you are unconsciously influenced by the thoughts of others. You will feel the effect in your solar plexus without knowing what is happening. Maybe you put it down to some physical cause. We are not suggesting, of course, that every upset of this nature is due to such emotional impact, but it sometimes happens. Then you need to protect yourself from thoughts that can penetrate your aura and affect this sensitive place, the centre at the solar plexus.

The way to protect yourself from receiving these arrows of thought is to steady your emotions, to control the emotional body. This is not easy, but it is essential if you wish to approach the higher planes, if you want to draw close to those higher brethren who are waiting to help you. You must prepare yourself to come within their aura. To do this, you must control your own emotional body, and this is where so many aspirants fail. They try hard, but their emotions are too unruly and so they keep themselves away from that calm, beautiful place where the master minds, the master souls dwell. We want you to think well about this because it is one of the very first lessons to be learned—the recognition of the reality of this emotional plane, of your own emotional, your feeling body.

You see from this that to protect yourself against the thoughts of people that disturb your emotional body you must seek the love of God, the love of Christ. You must pray for, and strive to be, this gentle love. In the degree that you can call forth that mild, peaceful, tranquil love in your heart towards life—not only to people but towards life itself, so that you are radiating love—you are encircling your aura with a white shield which is impenetrable by the world. Unwanted thoughts cannot penetrate your aura if you have sent forth love from the temple, the centre in your heart. If your emotions are controlled, calm and lovely, you cannot be affected, nor your mind be disturbed, by thoughts from the world. A master has complete control of circumstances through having gained mastery of his or her own being.

Those who want to develop the sixth sense of true intuition in order to work for the Master must rule their emotions. Sometimes the soul needs pain and suffering, both to develop the deeper emotions as well as to learn to control them. But the middle way is the way for the disciple—a ready response in the feelings to the sufferings of others, and to the spiritual influences which come to help the soul. Unruly emotions are a hindrance to the one who is seeking the development of the intuition.

The emotions are always symbolised by water. When water is turbulent, you get a false reflection. If the water is calm, clear and pure, you get perfect reflections from above. So when the soul has trained itself to be still and peaceful, it is receptive to true impressions, true feelings from spiritual worlds. Lack of mental control is the greatest hindrance in the Master's service. Peace is the achievement of controlled and wisely-directed emotion. The razor's edge upon which the disciple has to walk is to develop feeling, but also to control it.

The Perfect Flower

Imagine, if you will, a lovely gentle rose on the central altar of a temple, opening its petals to the sun. A rose is the symbol of a human heart fragrant with love. You may not often see hearts like this, but we do. We see many human hearts open to us and can inhale the perfume of sweet human love. Give out that same perfume yourselves. Withhold judgment and criticism. Remember the trials and the difficulties in another person's life which may make them irritable and sharp. Turn away wrath by gentleness and love, remembering that as you feel hurt and irritation, so may your companion feel too; and until you can feel with the feeling of your companion, you cannot be a master soul. The human way is to judge in haste the actions of others, but the divine way is to remain quiet and loving.

So, with this symbol of the rose in your midst, be very still, be at peace.... At this celestial level of consciousness, you should develop the power to receive truth, the power of feeling and imagination. If you feel the beauty of the heaven worlds, you are receiving divine truth through your intuition. This is how you can discriminate between the divine will and self-will. The disciple leaves all earthly things—mind, body, possessions, desires—to follow God. Having reached this understanding, you can safely rely upon your intuition. It all comes to these few simple words: 'Be still (in love) and know that I am God'.

Your whole life is lived within a concentration of cosmic forces, and like a magnet you attract to yourself conditions and powers like those you have awakened in yourself. All substance of whatever plane of life can be humanly moulded: by your thought, by your will, you can mould this substance into form. When you have really gained mastery over the physical body, the nervous system and the thinking—so that in all ways you can create the condition that the divine will within you wishes to create—then you are able, when you sit in meditation, to build round you 'the temple of the Golden Flower', exquisitely formed of spiritual or celestial substance. In meditation you are fully open like a beautiful flower, like the thousand-petalled lotus of the head chakra, or the many-petalled lotus of the heart chakra. You as a spirit are actually in that flower, and that flower builds up all around you in the form of a most beautiful temple, a spiritual temple. You are then in the temple of your own soul and spiritual world.

Through the blending of the intellect and the emotions the spirit is touched, the intuition reached. The feelings plus the thought-power open up the intelligence of the individual, as distinct from bare intellect, which cannot alone digest or deal with the food of the spirit. Controlled and wisely used, the emotions will so well interpenetrate the mind that the intuition and the divine intelligence can operate.

XI

SUBTLE BODIES

*And behold, a door was opened in heaven; and the first voice which
I heard was as it were of a trumpet talking with me; which said,
Come up hither, and I will shew thee things which must be hereafter.
And immediately I was in the spirit: and, behold, a throne was set in
heaven, and one sat upon the throne.*

Revelation 4 : 1–2

*To him that overcometh will I give to eat of the tree of life, which is
in the midst of the paradise of God.*

Revelation 2 : 7

IN THE FUTURE the sixth sense of intuition, which you are bringing
into operation, will become as natural as the other five senses. With
development of the intuition it is the heart centre and the brow chakra,
and lastly the crown centre, which are being awakened. The intuition is
unfailing only when it is selfless and when the human spirit is concentrating upon the Great Spirit.

There are records today of the visions of the saints. You have one
great example in your bible, in the book of Revelation. In these revela-
tions you have an illustration of the action of the true intuition, the
opening of the brow chakra, the rising of the soul and spirit of the seer

who is called John. He was carried up into heaven and there he saw what would happen. It was not much use his seeing without the interpretation of his vision. So you see that it is not only the opening of the vision: it is not only the seership, the seeing of pictures. It is the knowledge of how to interpret these pictures which the true seer must seek.

This is where we come down to life and to your human relationships, because it is your life, your relationships, your behaviour to each other, which is going to qualify you not only for seership but for the understanding, for the interpretation of what you see. You may be taken up into higher worlds, see many beautiful things; but if you do not have spiritual understanding they remain just figures and no more.

We have reached the next spiral on the path of evolution, and the aspirant today is not concerned with the monastic or ascetic life of old. He or she is called to mingle with humanity; to mingle with, and bring through into the minds of those he or she meets, the light of the ages. This same light must burn brightly in the aspirant, that its influence may send healing amongst men and women.

When your heart centre opens in love and kindness towards all creatures, it begins to grow and to expand, and can be seen by those with clear vision as a light radiating forth. Love God faithfully, and this light waxes and becomes brighter. By the power of this light miracles can be wrought, healings are performed, and all the spiritual beauty of human life is revealed. Development of this kind of sunlight within your own being enables you to develop what is loosely called clairvoyance or clear vision. Clear vision means an inward knowing. When you have this you know the truth, you recognize the love which exists in your brethren. You also understand their soul-needs. If you have not developed the light, you are so often deaf and blind to your brothers' and sisters' needs and to the yearning in their hearts. With clear vision you have an inward recognition of truth, not only in humanity but also in the scriptures of the great religions. You go right to the mark. You are direct in all your dealings, but are also aware of any hurt which your brother or sister may feel, and so you are careful and tender in action and speech.

The way to unlock the door of the kingdom, the heavenly mysteries, is by the way of meditation and love; and not by meditation alone, but by living in a simple, loving, caring way towards all creatures. The spirit must remain unaffected by the challenge—that is the word we will use—the challenge of matter, of the lower life. Strive to respond to beauty, and strive to feel love towards life. Let your heart be always in tune with the Infinite Love. If you can live in this manner, you will be living your meditation. You will be continually meditating upon that love which is the light, and to follow that light is the way to freedom from all limitations of the flesh. This is how the masters perform their miracles. They become saintlike in life. They dwell continually upon the thought of God, the purity of God, the love of God. They live in it. It comes to them and it goes from them. They become illumined through the development of the inner light—the light which is not only something beautiful in your heart, but a reality which permeates the very flesh which clothes your soul.

The light has to shine through matter and use it, control it, glorify it. If you do what you can to purify your own physical atoms by right thinking, right speech, right action, right living, judging no-one for what they do but looking to yourself; if you follow these precepts, then imperceptibly you will find that your consciousness is raised, and will uncover a happiness of which you have not dreamed. You will know peace in your heart, joy beyond earthly comprehension, and a gracious and gentle power which will enable you to make all crooked places straight, which will enable you to open the prison doors of your life.

Working with the Subtle Body

Psychic gifts are waiting to be uncovered in every soul, but every soul has to be trained and developed to the highest level so that the world they make contact with is the heaven world. In the course of evolution there are different periods of development. The first of them is the development of the psychic senses. Then that task is laid aside and there comes a period over which the mental body is built up. Next comes the time of spiritual development, and so on. All the time the complete being is gradually being constructed.

You like to have things cut and dried. You lay a foundation, then add the storeys one by one, but things do not happen quite like that in the world above the physical. If you can, try to picture this slow, gradual development of the soul and the growing God-consciousness of the spirit. The spirit, in its first pure essence, has developed neither self-consciousness nor God-consciousness. When it descends through the spheres and is clothed in matter, the individual self thus created holds within it the potential of this knowledge, this power. It all has to be unfolded through the process of physical life. So everyone—it does not matter who—has inner powers, but there are degrees of psychic and spiritual gifts. The psychic power is strong in people who live close to nature, for instance—who are much in contact with elementals. Their etheric body is much in evidence.

Radiating from the physical body, and interpenetrating it, is the etheric body, which is closely related to the nervous system. Then there is the astral body, and beyond the astral we come to the various levels of the mental bodies. To be more specific, there is a more earthly mental body, intimately related to the physical, but beyond this lower mental body is a higher one which, if you could see clearly, would appear as if it were a delicate, hair-like edge to the physical, and seems to put forth a line of light which emanates from the crown of the head. In the individual with a fairly high level of spiritual development, that line of light rises a long way. Sometimes its limit is not visible, but in some cases at the end of that line of light is another form, similar to this physical form, but most beautiful. This is what we call the higher self: the body of light. Everyone has such a body which develops in the course of their lives (notice that we say 'lives' and not 'life'). It is really the temple of the spirit. In the correctly and the well-developed soul, that spiritual body tends to become more and more beautiful. But it is the more earthy, etheric body, connected with the nervous system, which is the link with the other planes of life.

However, never reach outwards to find spirit people. That is a strange thing for us to tell you. Always go inwards to the heart. It is not in the brain, not in the solar plexus, but in the heart that you will make this true contact. From the solar plexus the planes of feeling and emotion and desire are contacted; from the throat and the frontal centre of the head, the mental plane; from the heart you reach beyond all these and go right to the centre of truth. This is why mystics were often humble, hardworking men and women. They had neither time nor opportunity for great mental achievement, but they loved their Creator, loved all things beautiful and gentle, loved nature and lived worshipping all living things. In this way they touched infinity, and became at one with the supreme spirit, the Christ-spirit.

Because someone has the power to see on the astral plane, it does not necessarily mean that that individual is spiritually evolved. The centre used in this type of clairvoyance and clairaudience is the solar plexus, which is a centre of the nerves. By your own reactions you know that. It is in the solar plexus, after all, that you feel fear and anxiety. Being able to see either etheric or astral forms does not always imply great knowledge or skill, but a particularly open solar plexus. This is neither good nor bad in itself, but remember that an individual in this condition is on rare occasions liable to obsession, for it is in the solar plexus that we find the voices are heard. When people say they are clairaudient they may only be receiving vibrations from the desire world, the plane of the lower and not the higher emotions. Such impressions can be troublesome. In the same way, someone who tells you that they only see spasmodically may see a vision which originates from the eye of the solar plexus, and is not the result of the trained clairvoyance of someone who has consciously opened the higher triangle of chakras. In other words, it is the revealing of a picture which is on the astral plane, and not under control.

We want to make it perfectly clear that you have the control key to your powerhouse. This is what people do not realize. They so long to get in touch with the other side that they will do anything. You might say that they tune in their instruments like radios, to various stations, and sometimes get a conglomeration of them going at the same time. It is noisy on some parts of the astral plane! If the chakra is open to that particular part, if the switch is on and the individual does not know how to control the switch, a terrible babble can come through, causing the derangement of the brain, and nervous breakdown.

The master key that you have within you is the Christ, or the spiritual power of the divine will that is in everyone. If ever you are troubled in this way, remember: let the I AM take control. Even that can be a misleading phrase, because many mistake their own desires, their lower nature, for the I AM—the Christ within. The Christ within arises and takes possession of the temple. You are the temple of Christ, and Christ commands the moneychangers and those making the noisy babble to leave the temple.*

Meditation as a Way to Spiritual Unfoldment

We are endeavouring by slow degrees to help humanity realize that the spirit life interpenetrates the physical and there is no 'here' and 'over there' in the way you think. There is no impenetrable barrier between matter and spirit, but an interpenetration; and the time comes soon when all will be touched by the magic and secret power which is spirit. This is already happening to some extent. The first step is being taken— in other words, the whole world is going through an initiation—a raising and an expansion of consciousness.

In this, it is good to make a habit not of dreaming your way through life, but of becoming very conscious at all times of the divine will and divine presence in the heart. It is easier to realize this presence when you train yourself to be tranquil in mind, to control the emotions and direct them wisely: not to repress them but to raise them onto a higher plane of love and service and kindness.

Let us take a moment for a word about kindness: having some spiritual knowledge, can you be sure that you weigh your words carefully? Do you consider the feelings of your brethren when you speak and act, not only in the big things of life, but in everyday conversation? Kindness must be spontaneous; the lips must be controlled by kindness, and

*John 2 : 14–15

always the thought, 'Will it hurt?' should be foremost. We can be cruel without knowing; without meaning to be cruel. Jesus said that cruelty was a great sin. If we are cruel in little things, can we wonder at the great outside world being savage and cruel?

So you see the importance of the daily meditation, the preparation for the day which sets you up in thinking before you speak and act, the importance of the control of the temper and emotions. This, my brethren, is the way by which you unfold the powers of clear vision and clear hearing. The power is then controlled in the solar plexus; it is stimulated in the heart, the throat and the head; it is directed at all times by the divine will—and you must cling, with all the power of God, to love and all the qualities of the Christ spirit. Then you will not be deceived; then you will not be inaccurate in what you see and hear. Your sixth sense is in the process of growth, and in time, even a seventh sense will be developed. Now, you have five senses which connect your soul with the physical plane; but the sixth sense is the first sense which connects your spirit with the physical plane. This is what you are striving after in your development, which must start with meditation.

You have heard us say before that the human body can be likened to a temple. Within this temple is an altar, on which burns a bright, clear flame. In your meditation seek this altar: try to imagine it, and bow your head in surrender before that altar flame within your own temple. You yourself are creating this glowing golden altar and the light upon it. It is real, for it is being generated by you, is arising in you; and thus you see it in the form of an altar blazing with light. This is not your imagination; it is what you are actually creating by your aspiration, your will, by concentration and direction of your thought. The flame which you see upon the altar may take the form of a rose with a brilliant jewel of light shining at its centre. If you see this in your meditation, remember that you are gazing upon your own heart chakra. Or, when you see the form of a lotus with its many petals, remember that you are gazing upon yet another of your own chakras. As you pray and meditate, as you kneel in devotion, you are causing the light to quicken in the chakras in your being, and causing them to open like the lotus.

The Chakras and Planetary Vibrations

Within the physical world, the physical body, is to be found expressed the profound mystery of the universe. You are all accustomed, whilst functioning through the physical body, to regard it as sufficient. You find it difficult to detach yourselves from it. After all, it is the vehicle through which you contact all the various experiences in life, pleasant or unpleasant, which bring sorrow or happiness, pain or joy. You register both physical pain and emotional suffering through the physical body, and many other influences.

In the great mystery schools the human body was chosen as the first study for the neophyte or pupil. Pictures and models of the human body were to be found in the inner temples of the mystery schools, with every part related to some sign of the zodiac. The astrological and astronomical knowledge of the wise teachers and priests enabled the neophyte to open his or her understanding and consciousness to respond to the universal powers directed upon him or her. Through knowledge of astrological influences operating on the various parts of the body, the pupil obtained understanding of true healing. The pupil recognized such influences as affecting his or her own life and developing the consciousness—the second aspect of being—and thus opened up a world sometimes described as the 'underworld' by the Egyptians, although here we will use the term 'soul world'.

Through contact with matter, via the physical body, the soul is acquiring the aspect of its nature representative of power. It learns through many incarnations to receive and use the creative power of life, and only through such earth incarnations does this God-creative power grow within its being.

As well as learning about the influences of the zodiac upon the soul's development, the pupil learnt of seven sacred centres in the physical body beneath which the ductless glands lie concealed, and learnt also that each centre was connected to or bore relationship to one of the seven planets. So the student responded to both planetary and zodiacal influence during physical life, both influences being concerned with the soul's evolution and development towards perfection.

When an individual has awakened, when he or she has learnt how to liberate the fire (or the creative power) within and has raised it up through the spinal column to the head centre, it will be as the raising from the dead of the Sun of life.* There are seven steps leading to the crown (or to the mountain top), and they can be noted on the spinal column. These seven, the sacred centres of the human body, are, as we have said, each related to a particular planet. Through the seven incarnations which form a cycle, the influence of one of the seven planets predominates during each of the seven incarnations. Each planet affects in turn one of the seven centres in the human body; and at the end of those seven incarnations, we arrive at a certain point on the spiral of evolution.

The particular ray or colour upon which you are progressing in this cycle is not necessarily that of the planet under which you were born in this day of life. The soul travels along a certain ray for a cycle of years, and during that cycle, according to the development of the higher bodies or vehicles, comes under other influences and vibrations. If one of the subtle bodies or vehicles which you were building required some particular vibration, then you would come under a specific ray in the process. If you were building a body which required another vibration, you would then come under another ray. You may have several incarnations under one particular colour, while developing the one vehicle. Then, when you were prepared to develop a higher vehicle, you would come under another vibration or colour.

We relate the head centre—that is, the pituitary and pineal glands— to Uranus and Neptune; to the influence of the finer and mystical forces. In the head centre, there comes a quickening of the clairvoyant vision. Uranus, as you know, is related to the new age, to the age of brotherhood, and Neptune to the influences on the higher planes.

When the red of Mars and of the lower centre, the genitals, and the powerful blue of the kundalini centre (governed by the Moon) are raised up, you will see the transmutation of those colours from the lower to

*The creative fire is described in Chapter VII, above, especially in the section headed 'The Plumed Serpents' (pp. 72–6). The chakras are also defined in that chapter.

the higher centres, wherein we find the indigo, and the violet. In their purest and highest form, the indigo and violet rays are the colours of Uranus and Neptune respectively. Both colours are associated with the head centre; and the two planets, Uranus and Neptune, have been discovered by your modern astronomers by the power of the mind. They have been discovered now because they have a special influence on humanity (and will have much more, as time goes on): because they are bringing the influence which is causing that transmutation from the lower to the higher triangle. It is interesting that the Uranian and Neptunian influences are influences upon the head centre. The balancing colour of green at the solar plexus is the halfway house, as it were, between the lower centres and the higher—the gateway through which the colours, or the powers, have to pass, to function in that higher triangle.

We relate Mercury to the throat centre. Mercury, the planet of the airy signs, influences the etheric body. The throat centre, as we have already said, controls, or has enormous influence over, the etheric body. You can clean the whole aura by direct contact with the throat centre. Mercury, then, controls the nervous system, and the etheric body, through the throat centre.

Yellow is suggestive of Mercury, but we also associate Mercury with the colour green. It is rather difficult to say where yellow ends and green begins. The yellow and the green we apply to the throat centre. Let us suggest a beautiful apple- or mid-green. At this centre it has a purifying and harmonizing effect upon the etheric, the astral and invisible bodies. The yellow also stimulates the higher mind, the pure intellect, and awakens the wisdom, because that yellow at the throat centre reaches the higher self of the person. The higher self, stimulated by the yellow at the throat centre, says to the weaker self, 'Do not be foolish and hold onto all that rubbish; let it go!'. The weaker or sick self in time reluctantly obeys.

Venus we link to the heart centre. It is sometimes said that the physical vehicle which the Christ is now using in His-Her work for humanity is the planet Venus. Venus is always associated with the colour pink, the colour of love. But we are going to give you a surprise. The mental aspect enters into the vibration of Venus also, and so we include the yellow ray.

We link Jupiter to the solar plexus. The mind of the emotions is to be found in the solar plexus, and we relate Jupiter to the emotional plane. The indigo ray is the one associated with Jupiter, but not Jupiter alone. Jupiter has a religious influence, and it brings beauty in many forms into the life. We associate indigo with the solar plexus centre; sometimes we say, for a ray of healing, 'blue to the solar plexus', because that again is a harmonizing colour. Jupiter brings harmony, as well as religious aspiration, so we find in indigo a suggestion of both green and the blue. We also associate indigo with the head.

Saturn, we relate to the spleen. The spleen is the gateway, the entrance for the light, the sunlight forces, into the etheric body. Saturn is the planet of regeneration, the planet which causes the light to enter the darkness of the physical life.

Green—a beautiful colour, set between blue and yellow—is a central colour. It is harmonizing, and is used extensively with blue in healing on the astral plane. Have you not heard from the beyond of newly-born souls who wake to find themselves lying on some grassy bank? Picture the exact shade; it would be a very clear and bright green, giving a strengthening and yet harmonizing effect. This green is the colour we attach to Saturn (but it is not the only connected colour).

We see in the planet Saturn a harmonizing and a balancing influence. Some of you may think otherwise! Pause a moment if you do, for Saturn is usually the great barrier between the lower and the higher worlds. When it can pass through the gateway of Saturn, then the soul can proceed to those higher realms of consciousness indicated by the pure blue—the spiritual power—and the indigo, indicative of the aspirational or devotional spirit, and then on to the ray of the violet which is a recognition of the full spiritual powers of the complete being.

Mars, we relate to the genital organs and to the base of the spine, for Mars controls the creative force, the life-force in the human body. The

Moon is also related to the lower genital organs, and the centre of life in the spine. And the Sun is linked to the apex of the triangle, to the head again.

The pivot of all these centres in the evolved type of person is the heart, which is like the sun of your universe. The heart centre breathes in and it breathes out. It absorbs—it takes in—sunlight. As the physical sun sustains life in the body, so the spiritual light and warmth behind that sun sustains the spiritual life in man.

Conceive these colours as very clear, bright, and pure; in the centre is a Star of white, representing the blending of all the colours into the one ray of white, indicative of the great light. The great white light is the first ray which you use, since it brings harmony. The white light dominates all else: it contains all the seven colours, or the rays upon which humanity evolves on the earth plane.*

Illumination

The brain is the vehicle through which the soul-consciousness expresses itself or works, and there is a part of the brain, the cerebellum, in which the soul 'resides'—the centre of the soul-consciousness. In front of this portion of the brain is that mystifying pituitary gland, which has a most important work. The pituitary gland is the 'eye' which receives the vibrations of the next step, of the etheric plane. The physical eye receives only the vibrations of physical light. The pituitary gland reflects the etheric light; and you should, when you focus your attention there, become aware first of light, and then of colour. Through that centre and the pineal gland the soul-consciousness is maintained.

The pituitary gland, situated behind and between the eyes, is linked with the pineal gland. These two glands are attached to the psychic centres of the etheric body, and in the course of development they will meet. Then development will follow on the crown of the head, until all the head centres are fully awakened and there is complete soul-consciousness. With growth and development of the soul-consciousness,

*For a further discussion of the colours and of all this topic, we recommend Joan Hodgson's book THE STARS AND THE CHAKRAS (White Eagle Publishing Trust, 1990)

the lower centres also become controlled, brought into union with the higher: the heart, throat and head centres.

We have an example of this in the crowning of our master Jesus at Calvary, with thorns.* They crowned him: the crown of thorns was pressed into the head, where this sacred centre is to be found. With the bridging or union of these two centres of spiritual power in the head— the pituitary and the pineal glands—there comes the illumination, or birth. This cannot be without the crucifixion of the lower self, the body, or without the resulting birth, or ascension, of the Christ into the heaven world—that sacred centre at the crown of the head—thus quickened into illumination.

Gradual development, control and use of these psychic centres will bring about that illumination and the complete soul-consciousness we earlier described—'marriage' or union between soul and spirit.† The soul represents the feminine aspect, and the divine spirit represents the male. The perfect union is the marriage of these two; or in another image the fusion of the higher triangle of the heart, the throat and the head centre, with the lower triangle of centres. Through this is brought about the perfect child of God, the perfect human being.

To be exact, the pituitary and the pineal glands are both closely associated with the creative centre at the base of the spine. Before there can come complete illumination, the birth of the Christ into fullness of life in every individual, the creative urge of the lower centre must resign its power to the head, to the 'mountain top'. Then the crown of thorns is changed into the circlet of gold. It becomes a crown of jewels giving sovereignty to the soul, and perfecting all.

In every group that is working for the brotherhood of all life, you who are participating are being attuned, as is the place in which you meet. You are sounding a tuning note, so that the forces of the higher worlds can be directed to that spot, to that group of people. Through these groups a note goes forth, not only on the earth, but on the astral plane: one which not only affects the people on earth, but also those awaiting incarnation, who are descending through the astral plane on

*Matthew 27 : 29 †See the section 'The Mystical Marriage' in Chapter II, pp. 25–8.

their way back to rebirth. Even though you feel of little consequence, the finer vibrations and the finer atoms in your higher vehicles are being attuned to be of use to the angelic hierarchies in their work for the future.

In the White Eagle Lodge we work on one specific ray to help each other to rise above the limitations of mortal life. Step by step this is taking place in us all, but so imperceptibly that it is not apparent, except perhaps in the atmosphere—which may be felt as a loving atmosphere—because the one foundation upon which these God-creative powers can be built, is that of devotion, of love.* And so, in everyday life, in human contact, there is growing a spirit of kindliness, of great true sympathy and love. The devotee feels the spirit of aspiration and devotion to the Master, to Christ. Love, gentleness, courtesy, never wearying in well-doing, always being ready to give help when help is called for (and when it is not specifically asked for, but needed): by these things the heart chakra or centre opens and the light streams forth from the heart. There comes, as it were, a light from within, shining through the eyes and radiating from the physical body. The rays reach down to within the individual as well as reaching up and out. As the rays go down they cause stimulation in the nerve centre at the base of the spine. The light from the heart stimulates and raises the serpent-power, the creative power, the Mother aspect of the deity; and as this power rises, step by step it stimulates the other centres of the body.*

We suggest to you that the only safe method of raising the serpent-power is through stimulation of the pure love ray, or the heart centre. Do not commence your endeavour by working upon the lower chakras

*The passage of White Eagle's teaching upon which the opening sentences of this paragraph are based has also been used in WALKING WITH THE ANGELS (White Eagle Publishing Trust, 1998), p. 46; reference to the discussion there takes the present subject further, for those who are interested in following it. However, the present section also dovetails with the one on the chakras in the November 2000 edition of White Eagle's SPIRITUAL UNFOLDMENT 1, Chapter II. There is another useful discussion of kundalini in the November 1999 edition of Grace Cooke's MEDITATION (written with White Eagle's guidance), pp. 45–46. Meditation, White Eagle says, along with service, is the safe and real way to develop and raise the serpent-power.

at all, but work entirely from the heart. By practice of love and wisdom this serpent-power is gradually stimulated; and then, through devotion to the Christ light, this power rises to the solar plexus, the heart, the throat, and finally comes an illumination called Christ- or cosmic consciousness. But first of all the foundation must be laid in daily life by the general attitude held towards the whole of life. That attitude must be positive, creative; it must see all the time good coming out of what is called evil and darkness. That is the foundation, and then more help can come through meditation.

When the power of kundalini is centred in the heart and the actions of the person come spontaneously from this centre of love, then we might say that the power of kundalini is absorbed into the Christ spirit and is manifesting through the Christ spirit, and is become the saviour of the man or woman instead of the destroyer.

The power of love arising in the heart is the Christ stimulation, by which kundalini saves instead of destroys. Therefore, the first signs of the arising of the kundalini fire is spiritual poise: control of speech, of the thoughts; general control and balance in life; a sense of great power. And when that power is under control and recognized by the neophyte or the student as the power of love and goodness, power which has to be used for the good of all and not for personal aggrandisement, then we know that the divine fire is rising and working in the individual.

To conclude, we should like to touch upon the inner meaning of the Tree of Life, and the Tree of Knowledge of Good and Evil. Here we bring to your mind the image of the human body. Can you see that each of you contains within the Tree of the Knowledge of Good and Evil? The spine can be likened to the trunk; and the two aspects of life—positive and negative, good and evil—rise up from the roots of the spine, blossom forth from the head and bring forth fruit. You can see a veritable Tree of Life in the circulatory system of the body, its stem, its branches, its intricate network. Within the individual is to be found both the Tree of Knowledge of Good and Evil and the Tree of Life. We see in this the possibilities of each human being's growth and regeneration from animal being to God-being, and the ultimate: the human tree, most beautiful of all, beneath whose wide branches of compassion and understanding humanity can shelter, and whose fruits of love and wisdom humanity can find.

XII

THE EAGLE OF JOHN AND
THE RAY OF BROTHERHOOD

I am come a light into the world, that whosoever believeth on me should not abide in darkness.

John 12 : 46

And the leaves of the tree were for the healing of the nations.

Revelation 22 : 2

SOMETIMES in our teaching we hark back to ancient Egypt. There is a reason for this. The age of the ancient Egyptian religion was the age of Taurus. Among the twelve signs, the sign opposite to Taurus is Scorpio. Scorpio is the sign of the scorpion or, in higher symbolism, the sign of the eagle—and we, you notice, use the name 'White Eagle'.

We want you to understand that 'White Eagle' is not just the name of a being. White Eagle is—shall we suggest?—a sign, an influence, a ray, a group; it is an aspect, perhaps, of a higher spiral of Scorpio. But the relationship which the eagle (or the scorpion), and the Taurean age of Egypt have with this present day, is to do with group work. For at this time there is brought back again to the earth the ancient wisdom which was practised and used in Egypt for healing and for building.

The Taureans are the builders, the builders of this grand cycle of life.

We stand now right on the cusp of the Aquarian Age—the age of the human being, of water, of spirit, and of brotherhood. To this influence can be added the influence of its opposite, Leo, for all ages are influenced by their opposites. Leo, the sign ruled by the Sun, brings strength and great force to humanity.

All these signs—Scorpio, Taurus, Leo and Aquarius—are fixed signs. In the four fixed signs you have the base of the pyramid, and the pyramid is the grand and ancient symbol of the whole of the world's life. There you have the history of this cycle of life built on the four-square; and the Sphinx, the eternal symbol to men and women of the way in, the entrance to the Temple. Through the Sphinx, or through the great Initiation, men and women will enter into the Grand Temple of the Sun—the Pyramid.

The white eagle represents Scorpio in its higher aspects. The human soul at certain times in its cosmic life—the length of which it is impossible to state—comes under the influence of the sign of Scorpio. These times bring special opportunity for spiritual development, for the unearthing of the divine spirit in the individual. The ancients say that initiation only takes place when the soul is under a powerful influence from Scorpio, or when the soul reacts to the heavenly stream of life consciousness known as the white eagle of St John.

So let us again draw your attention to the connection between the eagle and the one who was called the beloved disciple, St John. Before the Christian church was established, these two symbols of divine revelation—Jesus and John—were known and understood by the priests and the sages of the ancient wisdom. The two of them represent one ray, one lifestream, one aspect of the divine life which permeates humanity. According to our school of learning, the phoenix and the eagle are also synonymous. The phoenix is representative of the initiate, or the one who dies to the lower self and is reborn in the higher self or in the spirit; and the eagle is representative of the Word of God, which descended from the heavens and was clothed in flesh. The divine Word lies within the innermost of every son and every daughter of God.

St John himself came under the zodiacal sign of Scorpio—the teacher of the inner mysteries. St John is representing the age-long wisdom and is beyond your present human comprehension. He revealed in Revelation that esoteric spiritual power which lies within the being of all God's children. At certain times the ray of light from the same source as that which inspired John with visions of the future of human kind is present, we venture to say, in this Lodge.* Its symbol of the equal-sided cross within the circle is another ancient symbol of Wisdom, of the surrender of the self into the circle of eternal love, which alone brings true wisdom. The Star represents the Christ love. In this symbol of the cross within the circle with the Star at its heart, we have a representation of wisdom and love combined, which is to be realized by humanity in this new age—the age of Aquarius.

Brotherhood in Action

While each of you must develop your own lone path, you are never left alone. A paradox! Each of you is separate and you each have your own particular line of development and initiation, but nonetheless you are brought into a collective life, or brotherhood, through which you, in common with others assembled in that life, receive the benefit of the shared power and light drawn thither collectively by the souls. These collective initiations are governed and influenced by the planetary and zodiacal forces. Sooner or later the soul is made aware of the whole group. Up to that time it appears to travel alone, at least in its own consciousness. Suddenly, the time arrives when the individual becomes aware of its companionship with the group. This is of vital importance. The drawing together of the many into the group is governed purely by the karma of the individuals. Those constituting the group meet not once, but in many lives. Thus you have heard us say that many of you have been together in a group, or brotherhood, similar to this Lodge.†

*White Eagle of course refers to the White Eagle Lodge, where this teaching was given. For current addresses, see the last page of this book.

†This was said to those present when the talk was given, but must apply generally.

You forget, maybe; but that silent voice, which successive initiations will enable you to hear, will say to you: 'Yes, I remember, I know; I do not fully remember even now, but I have a feeling'. Oh, how valuable are these feelings! The angels help human evolution through feeling. The feeling comes, then, that you have met your brother or your sister before; that you are in familiar surroundings. It is vague; you do not understand. How many people enter a place such as this Lodge and say: 'I feel I have come home!'. To the outer mind this appears only imagination, but the true self within recognizes a memory, perhaps of an Egyptian or Atlantean incarnation ... of a life many, many years ago. They have been searching and searching ... for what? For association with a true spiritual group.

The ray of truth and light by which the beloved John received his book of Revelation was directed to earth from the very throne of God, and it is same ray as the one which calls you, as individuals, onto the path of brotherhood. All souls preparing for initiation need therefore to recognize the needs of their brothers and sisters, and become aware of the way in which the group soul cooperates. When initiation brings expansion of consciousness to the candidate, enabling the soul to become aware of its particular group, it no longer lives to itself, for itself, but recognizes that every thought, every action concerns not itself alone, but will inspire and help, or hurt or degrade (as the case may be) all the members of the group. Therefore the responsibility becomes very great. The candidate is no longer free, so to speak. He or she has never been free, actually, but thought him- or herself so, and thought that the result of personal actions came upon him- or herself alone. Now the soul is no longer free, because it is aware that it cannot injure any brother or sister in the group without the whole group being affected, including itself. In truth, none really can act only of or for themselves. They may pride themselves on isolation, but it is impossible to injure another without injuring the self. The point we are trying to convey is that after initiation into this awareness of the group, the responsibility of the soul becomes vastly greater.

This plan of initiation was introduced to humanity in the Atlantean period. It was a system of initiation instituted by the great beings after humanity's choice of the path of self-will. It has been very successful. At certain times in human evolution there has come an outpouring of power, when certain great teachers have come to help humanity towards initiation. We touch, of course, on the coming of the most recent world teacher, Jesus of Nazareth. Ever since the outpouring of the life of Jesus, humanity has been preparing for a further expansion of consciousness. It may seem hardly possible that people could be so blind, so foolish, so dense, as to spend incarnation after incarnation in darkness, even after the baptism of the earth by the revelation of Jesus Christ, but it has been so. And before the next manifestation there will be a quickening of the spirit, the initiation of many, and the casting-off of the bandage which has blindfolded the individual for so long.

At present, you are going through the preparation for this world initiation, and there will be a great step forward in brotherhood and goodwill, and a development of knowledge of all the seven rays upon which humanity is evolving. If you will consider the effects of the seven rays of spiritual activity on the earth, you will recognize that an advance is made upon each one of them, not in turn but almost simultaneously: an advance not only of the individual but of the group to which the individual is attached, of the nations, and of the whole world.

A great opportunity is now being presented to you—and to all humanity. You are the builders of the new age. It is not good for you to sit down complacently. For as surely as humanity (or the western world) settles down in complacency, there will arise in another part of the world a powerful force which will again challenge that complacency, and make humanity rise to the occasion and give true service to the vast human family. The conditions of the world today are stimulating and drawing out this goodness, which lies within every living soul, and which quickens the consciousness of those who are now turning their faces upwards. You will see, in years to come, more of what you are already beginning to feel in yourselves: a transmutation, a quickening of the vibrations of life. First of all comes the transmutation of your own individual atoms, and the consequent lightening and refining of the body. What applies to the individual applies also to the world at large.

You look back over two thousand years, which you think is a long time. It is nothing. Jesus was the messenger heralding the new age of Aquarius, and it has taken human kind two thousand years even to penetrate the truth of the teaching and the wisdom which Jesus brought. Now humanity has to assimilate that truth—to become as the Master directed; and individuals have to put into operation those laws of the divine spirit ... the law of love and brotherhood, the law of divine healing which Jesus lived. From the heart of Jesus flowed continually the radiation of a pure white magic. Any human heart can still receive this same radiation from the heart of the Christ, and if that heart keeps pure and joyous it can in turn radiate light and healing to all the world.

Realizing the Christ Star

The Pole Star had, in the beginning, a mighty influence upon human life. It receives the influence of all the planets concerned with the evolution of life on earth. It is like a magnetic star, and through it the rays are directed on earth's humanity. The light and the power of this Pole Star fell upon the very early peoples of what we might call the Polarian Age, the age when people were directly under the Star, an age of light and brotherhood. But, with what is known as the Fall, people chose, of their own freewill, a certain path, which caused the whole of the life of the earth to change. It caused the spiritual magnetic pole to be a little out of alignment, which has brought all manner of sorrow and suffering, and so-called evil; but humanity is learning once again to return to polarisation with that Pole Star. This Star which you follow—the six-pointed Star—is really symbolical of that Pole Star above, to which all humanity will learn in time to be polarised, so that the direct rays of this great Star will fall again upon humanity, bringing brotherhood and light and the perfect age.

We draw your attention to the symbol of the Christ Star—built up, created, as a beautiful, blazing Star pulsating with light. The rays stream forth afar and the symbol is ever-living; its rays are continually going out, illumining the earth. What is the origin of this Star? Insofar as this particular manifestation is concerned, it is the result of a long period of God-thought, good thought, loving thought, constructive thought, which has been sent forth by those working on earth and in spirit. This concerted effort, this power which has been going out for so long, creates this form. It is, however, far more than a thought-form, and is being projected out over the world and into the invisible spheres which surround this planet.

The symbol of the six-pointed Star is to be found in age-old esoteric teaching and used by brotherhoods all over the world, in many ages. The six-pointed Star is the most beautiful symbol of the perfectly-balanced soul, the soul whose head is in the heavens, whose faculties are quickened to receive the light from above, and whose feet are firmly planted upon the road of earth, which the soul traverses with one object in view—to find and give true happiness of the spirit. Whichever way you turn it and whichever way you use it, it remains the same: perfectly balanced, a focal point (if held with love, concentration and devotion) to attract the angelic hosts from the Christ spheres who work ceaselessly for the Christ power to manifest on earth. Where the Star shines by the will and through the love of earthly men and women, the effect over chaos and disorder, war, and all the evils in the world can be truly magical.

The Star is not only a great cosmic power, it is also a tender, loving, guiding power; a protecting power in your own lives. If you can surrender yourselves to the sweet and lovely Star radiance, you will find that your pathway will be one of light and happiness and gentle peace. The Master knows your fears and your sorrows, and you will receive the comfort, the guidance and the love that you need as you go to him, as you go into the Star. Nothing matters more than this spiritual life in you. It is the key to heaven, heaven on earth, as well as the heaven world after death.

When you send out the light of the Star, do not merely force it out from your brow chakra. Open yourself in humility, sweetness and love to the Christos, to the one who is called Christ—the human being who is made perfect—the perfect Son or Sun of God. When you want to send out the light of the Star, try first to get that feeling of love in your heart. Jesus said so simply, *Love one another*. So we love God. We raise our thoughts to the apex of the golden triangle and visualize there the glorious Star. We hold that Star—that point of light—and in that point of light, right in the centre of that perfect, geometrical, six-pointed Star, we may hold the image of anyone we desire to help. Or we may just hold the Star and see its rays shining forth. If you do this properly and in sincerity, you will succeed not only in helping your patients and helping the world by sending out light into the darkness of matter; but you will, at the same time, be developing within yourself that lovely Golden Flower, of which we have spoken, and be living in the Star Temple.

This is the secret: to live, to know and to be in the consciousness of the Infinite Love and Light, and to live for spirit and not for matter. Matter is secondary; spirit is the first and foremost in human life, and to live rightly you must live to develop the consciousness of the Great White Light or the Christ within yourself. Not in the brow, but in your heart, and in the thousand-petalled lotus at the apex of your triangle. Work always with this higher triangle, and the Star. The triangle is in the Star—your triangle on its base, and the balancing triangle penetrating, coming down to unite and form the Star ... you are in it, and you have to become aware that you are in it, and to develop the consciousness of the power of this Star to perform miracles. But remember, it is not your will when a miracle is performed. It is God's power, it is God's will. God is the light in humanity and God alone gives or withdraws according to His–Her wisdom. We hope you understand that, and will not force what you think ought to be done. Surrender to God's will in all things.

XIII

INNER DEVELOPMENT AND OUTWARD CHANGE

Thou shalt love the Lord thy God with all thy heart, and with all thy soul, and with all thy mind.... Thou shalt love thy neighbour as thyself.

Matthew 22 : 37, 39

Our Father which art in heaven, Hallowed be thy name.

Matthew 6 : 9

Though I walk through the valley of the shadow of death, I will fear no evil: for thou art with me; thy rod and staff they comfort me.

Psalm 23 : 4

Which now of these three, thinkest thou, was neighbour unto him that fell among the thieves?

And he said, He that shewed mercy on him. Then said Jesus unto him, Go, and do thou likewise.

Luke 10 : 36–37

WHEN WE tell you that human kind has a glorious future and that within each individual lie the most wonderful possibilities, you find it difficult to believe. In olden days, when much of humanity was really living in a dark age, religion painted a picture of a heaven that was to come after death; that is to say, the Christian church promised a heaven which was certain so long as the person had faith and belief in its doctrines.

We do not speak of a life divorced from this earth when we tell you of a life of beauty, of glory, of perfection; a life of happiness, harmony and beauty. We speak of the life which can first of all be realized by man–woman within his–her being, and secondly on the outermost plane. Heaven can indeed be realized on earth.

There are several ways in which this can happen. The human spirit can become so radiant, so dominant over the physical life, that it can penetrate to the higher realms of consciousness which you think of as heaven. Instead of this heavenly state being in some far-away sphere up in the clouds, this heaven can be found here on earth. It is possible for a man or woman to become so attuned to truth, to his or her true being, as to see beyond the veil of materialism into that land of light which is the land of the spirit. If the individuals desire this, it is necessary for them to unfold their spiritual qualities. Only when these spiritual qualities are unfolded is man–woman raised up by the Christ spirit so that he–she can behold and actually take part in a life of unimagined beauty—harmonious, holy, healthy, peaceful—but also a life full of energy and activity and service, and at the same time a life which can be enjoyed in tranquillity. All this would seem almost impossible, particularly during the dark years of the past century, but the darkness will lift and the sun will shine again.

Most surely, the answer to every human problem lies in the divine mind. Until all human beings can rise above self and make contact with that divine mind, they will not receive the guidance for which they long. Even those with some knowledge of these spiritual truths often forget the source of wisdom, or the centre of truth which will always respond, if only they will prepare themselves and learn to go to that centre for their answer.

The great need you have at present is to understand that you have an inner spiritual life and an outer worldly life. It is essential that all of you begin to develop your spiritual part. You have pure spirit within your own being. You are all on the earth to develop your spirit, which lies buried beneath many coverings, physical, mental, emotional. There is something very grand within all humans. You have been given tools in this life to enable you to shape that perfect figure of the Son, the Son of God, the Christ Being. You do not really grasp that within you is something more precious, more beautiful, more wonderful than you have ever conceived. Occasionally you hear of a reflection or a manifestation of that glory coming in flashes through great people, and of course through those whom you call masters. You see through them the radiance, the glory, the beauty of the divine life. You think to worship, but never to draw near to that Being. You worship from afar instead of taking hold of yourself and working to perfect your own character and your own soul; so that it becomes fitted for that same divine spirit to manifest through you to all creatures. This is the whole purpose of your life.

In this new age into which you are advancing, there will be great stimulation of both the materiality and the spirituality of the human race. There are already a large number of souls in incarnation who, consciously or unconsciously, knowing or unknowing, have come to be pioneers for this new age. We would have you realize that however simple, however obscure your own life, you have a very special charge. You have come back to earth for a special purpose; you have come not only to develop your divine consciousness but also to pioneer the pathway which will become the path for all who will follow. You cannot help but develop your own character and divinity if you are truly serving others. At the same time, do not concern yourself too much with your own growth and development, so long as you have a true outlook. All you have to do is to obey spiritual law, and then you will find yourself on a path.

This path is the path of all pioneers of the spirit. Those in incarnation today are having a hard time, for they are preparing for the coming at a later period in the Aquarian Age of many brothers and sisters of the Great White Lodge. Angel beings, too, will draw near. Men and women will walk and talk with angels, but remember that it takes an angel to recognize an angel, a god to recognize a god, so until men and women have developed the necessary qualities within themselves, they remain unconscious of the presence of angels or of gods. A perfect law is working through life and no-one can escape either reward or suffering, either joy or pain. You are a magnet and you attract to yourself that which you are yourself. The vibrations you create within yourself are very powerful. They draw to you similar vibrations.

How can you break through this darkness which envelops you? Only by developing the divine will in your heart—the will to obey the law of the Christ life. How are you going to develop this will? Well, we will tell you of a very simple measure, so simple that you may take little notice of what we say—but every day and all day seek to obey God's command to *love the Lord thy God with all thy heart, and with all thy soul, and with all thy mind ... and ... thy neighbour as thyself.* 'Thy neighbour as thyself': this is a very subtle command. It does not say love your neighbour more than yourself—but your neighbour *as* yourself. Love the Lord thy God with all thy heart, with all thy soul and with all thy mind, and thy neighbour. That is all. That is the law. But it is not so simple.

If you are going to obey the law you have to do it physically, mentally, emotionally, spiritually. This means you have got to command your thoughts. You have to bring the divine will into operation. You have to will that you will the will of God not only for yourself but for all life, so that you recognize the omnipotence which overshadows the world and also is in charge of your own life.

You are all waiting—yes, waiting—for something to happen. Each one of you individually is hoping for a brighter future. We want you to learn the lesson that eternity is now, the future is now. There is neither past, nor present, nor future as separate periods of time: all is within the soul's embrace now. It is your reaction to the now which makes your future. Never look to the future and anticipate this, that, or the other. Live today, with God, and no future can hold for you any greater joy than is yours today. Many folk spend their days waiting for something to happen, for something to turn up. This is to live in fear, and today we would help you to see the foolishness of this. Live today. Live and be at peace, and you have entered your kingdom of heaven.

With regard to the problems of the age, people nearly always try to solve them from a purely material standard. We see so much sorrow in the world, and so much fear. Men and women are indeed full of fear— fearful of their brothers, their sisters, and fearful for themselves. We would speak particularly about this, because fear corrodes and consumes the happiness of a vast number of human beings. There is fear of life generally, fear of the future, fear of loss, fear of ill-health, fear of separation from loved ones, and above all, fear of death. Fear seems to be the greatest enemy of human kind, and the first thing that a human being must strive for is to overcome fear.

Anxieties can crowd and almost submerge the mind by the turbulence of emotions involved. When fear threatens to overwhelm you, enter the quiet temple within and, by strength of will and spirit, control the emotions. Raise your heart in supplication: 'My Father ... Divine Mother'. Do not dwell any further upon your trouble; it is now in God's keeping. Come, with a full heart, into the circle of God's love....

'Father, Mother ... you who are in heaven, *hallowed be Thy name.*' This is a state of perfect peace and happiness: 'You are my Father– Mother, and You can raise me up to be with You in heaven. Your tranquillity and peace alone can bring rest into my heart and soul.'

In the light of our Father, nothing can hurt. We may go through the valley of the shadows and He is with us. His rod and His staff, they comfort us. Therefore open your inner sanctuary, and allow the power of the Spirit to guide you tranquilly down the river of life. In tranquillity: but this does not mean that you lose your own responsibility or need for action. When the way is revealed, God may call for decision and action, not passivity.

You who fear for material needs, remember God's love is omnipotent. God knows! For you, we say, take courage; step forward on life's path like sons and daughters of God. He–she has prepared the sustenance, the food, the experience which you need on life's journey, so that you may grow and evolve.

The Power of Thought

We cannot too strongly emphasize the power of thought. You think that thought is something private—that no-one can read human thoughts; but truly there is no covering to thought. It is heard, it is seen, and moreover it often has a dynamic power, as you have yet to learn. Your thoughts are either helping the world to enlightenment, or are holding back the progress of humanity. Thought can create good health and thought can also heal, but thought can introduce pain and disease, and can disrupt and destroy the bodily, mental and human soul-life. Science is only on the outermost fringe of comprehension of the power of thought. Thought can do anything in the world. Thoughts of anger, fear and hate form the root of all suffering and of wars. Thought can also bring forth beauty and harmony, and brotherhood, and all else that men and women long for. We know that by seeing only good, by creating good, by positive thought, we can help to bring about that which is desirable and good.

As you progress on your path it will be clearly demonstrated to you that what you think you become; the vibrations set up by your thoughts are making an impression on the higher ether. You register something on that higher ether, and thereby attract to yourself corresponding waves or forces, which again, when they return (if you still pursue your path of wise thinking, or unselfish service to others) will create certain conditions in your life. The law, working in the human mind and soul, creates conditions of life and brings to individuals (if they are working in the right way) these things for which they pray and hope. But it is not only a matter of thinking what you want. That is only a small part of the picture. The real truth is that you wish to work with God to create harmony, beauty and healthfulness, holiness and happiness, not only for yourself, but for all human kind. It is this motive of creative love which gives power and life to your thoughts and prayers.

We want you to realize that your thoughts are drawn, through magnetic vibration, towards other great thought-streams—both positive and negative. All positive thoughts—by this we mean thoughts which are good, uplifting and constructive—go forth from you and by the law of attraction align themselves to great streams of thought which are positive, which are good, which belong to the White Light. Thoughts of cruelty are, in their turn, used to swell the great streams of dark or negative thoughts. Oh, how much cruelty there is in life through thoughtlessness! Thoughtlessness can cause much suffering. Thoughtfulness brings love, joy, hope and courage. Your thoughtfulness, whatever form it takes, is a contribution to that great stream of White Light upon which humanity depends for its very existence.

We look out upon the world knowing all these simple truths that we have been taught by the masters of all time, and aware that our work here is to gain mastery over ourselves. We look out into the world and see conflict. We see many varying points of view which may, according to our standard, seem right or wrong. One truth is certain, and this is that above all is the great ruler—the Great Spirit—and every one of the children of the Great Spirit is as dear to Him–Her as we are; and that the Great Spirit looks out upon the world desiring only that His–Her children should grow in spirit, and so find the happiness which the Great Spirit desires for them. God wishes all men and women to grow in beauty of spirit, all to have opportunity for expansion and growth— not just a few here and there, but all God's children. God has created man and woman, put them in a world of infinite promise, given them infinite possibilities within. Only you yourself can develop yourself, and nothing can stay anyone from developing those infinite possibilities, since the Infinite Spirit is all love, truth, wisdom, gentleness and brotherliness towards all creatures.

Seek the will of God, and not self-will. Let all nations seek the divine will for the whole earth. No country need be anxious if it puts into operation the law of God in all its dealings. We know that many problems will arise, but we still maintain that the spiritual law is the way of peace. Humanity, however, has yet to give this spiritual law an opportunity; and instead, people have many excuses and reasons ready why spiritual law should not be applied. This is nevertheless the only answer, and so we say: in your own life *seek first the kingdom of God*. Go into the silence; seek there, and then when you have found it, let it manifest in your own lives. Put aside all temptations; harbour no unkind words or thoughts. In their place, let there be consideration and thoughtfulness, remembering the difficulties that all people, including yourselves, have to encounter. This is the law of Christ, and this is what Christ did through his servant Jesus of Nazareth. *Go, and do thou likewise* and you will have nothing to fear. Instead, you will unfurl your wings and rise into the world of great joy, light and peace.

Every time a destructive thought comes into your mind, therefore, dismiss it at once; because it is with this accumulation of destructive thought that the mental body of human kind as a whole is being fed with ideas which create destructive weapons and evil ways of destroying life. We want to show you this clear picture: on the one side, see the creative power used for good; while on the other side, there is the array of dark, destructive thought which finds entry into the minds of strong intellects to create methods of destruction, as well as stimulating the destructive human passions and emotions. What we in spirit are all working for is to bring about harmony and balance in human life, and you too can discipline yourselves to think and create forms of goodness, beauty and harmony.

Now the destructive power of evil is necessary on the earth, for there is a great deal to be cleared away—outworn ideas, and outworn methods in many different departments of life. To this end the powers are working to clean up—or, shall we say, destroy—because when a condition has served its purpose it must be absorbed, it must go, and this is the value of the destructive element in life. We would give you a true perspective of the value of destruction—of the clearing away of old methods and old ideas, and of making ready for the coming of the good, the true and the beautiful. This is what we mean when we say that the balance must be maintained.*

*Just as White Eagle's teaching elsewhere seems to run alongside the Buddhist boddhisatva principle, and at others alongside the Hindu goddess of compassion, Avolakitesvara, here it seems to be the Hindu deity Shiva, creator and destroyer, who is present, unannounced.

At the beginning of the Aquarian Age, the influence of the Mother aspect will be seen in all places, in all planes of life. Let us bear in mind, however, that the Mother-aspect of God is dual and destroys as well as creates. Before the new age of Aquarius can fully be ushered in, there has to be a breaking-down of old conditions. We witness this breaking down everywhere; but those hurt in the process need healing. Indeed, they must be healed in order to bring forth the new, beautiful age of the spirit.

The power of thought can indeed work miracles, but this will itself bring up questions in your mind. You will have to remember that humanity is evolving on a spiral and its evolution proceeds in cycles. Men and women have to learn to use their occult power—their God-power—with the Christ love in their hearts. Until they have learnt to do this they have to suffer any pain which wrong usage of the God-power will cause. The masters we have been talking about have learnt to use this power only in love and in service to their companions, or to humanity, and this is what has to be learnt by men and women in the course of their slow spiritual evolution.

What we have to give you is a message about your opportunity to use your own thought-power to help humanity instead of to hurt it: in order to help yourself instead of to hurt yourself. All people have the power to think constructive God-thought, not only at certain times, but as a natural habit. Instead of complaining, 'Oh, what a beastly day!', try to think: 'Oh, another God-given day. How good is the rain! Mother earth needs the rain. How good is the cold. Mother Earth needs the cold to cleanse herself in preparation for spring'. Always see the best in everything and in everybody. Instead of thinking: 'Oh, so and so means to hurt me; so and so is wrong; I am right', realize that whatever another soul is doing, your attitude and your thought must be tolerant, kind and good.

We are preaching a gospel of perfection; we know this very well, but then you have the seeds of perfection already in you. You do not need to think of yourself. All you have to do is to live your days, love everything and everybody; just breathe love, live love, think love—and then attacks cannot penetrate your armour. Remember your thoughts; keep a check on them. You will gradually re-create your conditions, re-create your life. In our world young souls are taught how to use this power; buildings are created in our world by thought. You would be surprised, and amused too, at some of the efforts of the young to build, to create a building in our world: they get it out of proportion because they are not used to using thought-power in the right way!

Those of you who are used to meditation will realize the possibilities of creative thought, God-thought, good thought. Perfect thought creates perfect form, and you will create a perfect life in time. Do not habitually think about war or other terrible things. See the creation of good as an outcome—always, always, always—and you will be actively helping to bring about those conditions.

There are many who will say, 'But how is this possible when there are disagreeable conditions to contend with on the physical plane?'. It is possible, but it does need self-control, and control of all kinds of thoughts: disturbing, distracting, and diseased thoughts. You say you cannot help your thoughts rushing in—they come before you realize it. Well, that is true. But you can, in time, control the uprush. It cannot be done instantly. You cannot sit down one morning and say, 'I will not have any unwanted thoughts today'. It is not quite as easy as that! It may take a long time, and even several lives, to gain this poise of spirit—to achieve this domination of the earthly mind by the pure spirit, the divine in you.

Do not be discouraged, but start right away to follow the plan we have outlined for you. Make it habitual to welcome and respond to thoughts of purity, gentleness, kindliness and goodwill. Make no mistake, this does not mean that you must go about your daily lives in a pious and sanctimonious attitude. This is the last thing we would advocate. Be natural; be generous in thought; keep constantly the reminder in the heart of the presence of the Christ—the noble and perfect child of God—the Cosmic Christ, who manifested so beautifully through the master Jesus.

Lastly, we would add: it is not only a matter of thinking what you want—that is only a small part of the picture. The real truth is that you wish to work with God to create harmony, beauty and healthfulness, holiness and happiness, not only for yourself but for all human kind. It is this motive of creative love which gives power and life to your thoughts and prayers. This is the work of brotherhood.

Spiritual Growth is the Result of Perseverance

If you meet what you call failure, do not despair and say, 'I am not there yet'. The very fact that you are trying shows you are at one level already there. If not, you would not be trying. The fact that you can create a longing and set your vision on an ideal shows that you are ready.

Remember that when you are on this path the graph goes up and down. The soul is bound to be carried up to the heights and bound to descend again. At times you will feel full of spiritual ecstasy and can do anything; and there will be times when you feel hopeless. Never, never mind. Hold on with a loving heart to your ideal and to your Father–Mother God, the Parents who are watching over you, who understand their child because they have given you birth. Keep on persevering with your everyday life and with your set lessons, thereby bringing this light within into conscious operation, so that the very cells of your body become finer. This is what is happening in the world. Spirit—God—is continually moulding, purifying, raising the world's vibrations.

Let us remember that only a part of the soul comes back with each incarnation, and not the greater self; what incarnates is only like a feeler, like an arm put forth to gather more experiences into the greater self. So, if you lack opportunity for certain lessons, it does not mean that you do not need those lessons, but that you have come back with a set purpose, and that the other lessons are not on your horizon for this particular incarnation. You are set to gain experience on one particular line. Whether you are developed on other lines, or whether your neighbour is developed on these lines or not, you cannot tell. How impossible it is for you to judge your companion! You do not know his or her soul; unwittingly, you may be entertaining a great being in your home! You do not know. Some people have peculiar ways of showing their greatness, we admit, but in any person only one 'feeler' of the real self is coming through; you do not know what the higher consciousness has stored within it.

When the soul has acquired all the lessons necessary; when it has attained a degree of completeness, it puts forth a more complete presentation of itself, and then you are able to see and recognize a master, an adept, an initiate. That soul is putting forth, not its entire self, even then, but the greater proportion, because it is ready to serve humanity in its own particular way. But do not think that the younger soul is giving its true nature. That remains in the higher consciousness.

You know, it does not matter very much who is a great soul and who is a young soul. We do not think it matters at all. Do not worship one who you think is great, but endeavour to love all, both great and small, young and old. Love them all. All are the same in God's sight.

Is it possible to remain aware of the higher consciousness which you have, all through the working day? It is possible, but difficult. It comes with continual aspiration and self-discipline. As you progress on the path of continual meditation, you get two levels of consciousness— that is to say, you may be engaged in everyday things on the surface, but beneath the surface there is always this consciousness of the universal divine love. You become aware beneath the daily consciousness all the time.

A time will come, though, when every soul will be aware of its higher life and of its true self. Then it will be able to see the two selves in contrast—the limited earthly self and the higher, heavenly and eternal self. As development proceeds, the higher self becomes stronger and more in evidence in everyday life. Then problems and difficulties no longer overwhelm the soul; they keep to their rightful place. The soul develops vision, not only of God and of heavenly things, but also of earthly things. It sees things in their true perspective, and its sensitivity enables it to penetrate the ethers and to receive radiation from the higher worlds.

To achieve what we have told you you can find, you must work steadily onward. And we tell you that if you can put into practice in your daily life one iota of what you hear or read, flowing through from us in words, you will do very well indeed!

When a measure of control has been earned, when these earthly tests have been safely passed, the time always comes for a person to be summoned into the great Hall of Initiation. The soul is led by the guide through many intricate ways, many dark passages—which is what you are going through now in your earth life. You do not know where your road leads, nor when you will turn the corner, nor what you will find round it. Human life is really a passage through which the being—man or woman—is being led by its guide, not only in one incarnation, but through many.

At long last the soul comes into some gracious and beautiful place, and is led up to the blazing altar of light—so strong that it may be that the eyes must be veiled. But at the end of the great ceremony the eyes are no longer blindfolded. They behold the blazing Star, the Star of six points: six outer points, but with one central point, seven points in all. This seven-pointed Star corresponds to the seven great rays of life, the seven rays which come from the seven angels round the throne of God. Through a long, long journey each soul has also been learning, training, gaining power to send forth the light from every one of the seven sacred centres in its own body, and to draw upon the seven sacred planetary forces which work through each sign of the zodiac. Perfected man–woman not only sees that blazing Star at his or her initiation, but realizes that he or she in truth is that Star.

A Higher Level of Being

The higher self is composed of very fine ether and is pulsating with light, which as you develop will begin to shine through the chakras in the etheric body, the 'windows of your soul'.

When this divine fire is brought into full operation so that all the chakras are active as God intended, then the whole body will be in a state of ascension. We mean by this that the whole body, although still of a physical nature, will be functioning on a much higher plane of consciousness than it is at present. At present it may be in a dark state, but when the divine fire is kindled and active, then the body will be quickened in vibration and will be light and beautiful. It will approach the standard achieved by the God-beings, the Sun-beings, who walked this earth in the beginning of its creation.*

You are here to use physical matter, and not allow it to dominate you. You are here; you are light; and *you* have to shine out through the darkness. You have to use your physical life and raise it, to transmute the heavy atoms of the physical body.

Within you lies the power to change the very atoms of your body, for the physical atoms are the spiritual atoms. These tiny sparks of light are the power behind all visible form. These atoms can be changed by the command of God. The whole of life is under the direction and command of the Great White Light.

Healing is the intake into the body of the eternal Sun, the light. If you can call upon this light, breathe it in, if you can live consciously in this light, it will actually control the cells of the physical body. The body is so heavy, material life so strong—but do not forget the power of God to recreate the living cells of your body.

When we said earlier that there would be a new planet born from the heart of the Sun or Son, we meant that from every life will be born a new world. This is beyond your comprehension at present, perhaps, but remember that you are all sons and daughters of God, and will become gods, from whom will be born a new world.

As they grow in spirit, the people will no longer fear death. The people will not even know death, because they will be quickened to life in the spirit. Death with all its morbid trappings will be a thing of the past. When men and women have finished their period of service they will withdraw from the physical body to a place for refreshment in the heavens, still retaining full consciousness of life in all its fullness, both on earth and in the spiritual sphere. Death will be overcome by the

*This passage has been taken from White Eagle's book HEAL THYSELF (White Eagle Publishing Trust, 1999 edition, p. 62) and the one that follows it, from THE SOURCE OF ALL OUR STRENGTH (White Eagle Publishing Trust, 1999 edition, p. 29).

spiritual life. Death will be swallowed up in victory, in immortality; because when men and women learn to live by the true spirit, recognizing in each other the same spirit as that within themselves, they will know that there is no separation by death.

XIV

THE MASTER SOUL

[Simon] saith unto him, Yea, Lord; thou knowest that I love thee.
[Jesus] saith unto him, Feed my lambs.

John 21 : 15

By their fruits ye shall know them.

Matthew 7 : 20

The Father that dwelleth in me, He doeth the works: not I.

John 14 : 10

I and my Father are one.

John 10 : 30

The prince of this world cometh, and hath nothing in me.

John 14 : 30

Man shall not live by bread alone, but by every word that proceedeth
out of the mouth of God.

Matthew 4 : 4

Ask, and it shall be given you; seek, and ye shall find; knock, and it
shall be opened unto you.

Matthew 7 : 7

Am I my brother's keeper?

Genesis 4 : 9

WILL YOU ENDEAVOUR to cultivate the manner of thinking very widely and universally as we speak about the idea of a master? Do not try to put labels on people, and do not create idols of people, personalities. It seems to us that as soon as you confine the radiance of a spiritual being in a personality and you label him or her with a certain name, you are robbing that being of its true greatness, greatness which cannot be confined or limited to a human personality. There are some schools of thought who have found masters, and they have named them, and people sometimes ask us if these same masters are the only masters in the scheme of human evolution. And then again you will wonder who is *your* master.

We do not want to confuse any of you, and we do not wish to upset your preconceived ideas about the masters, but it is unwise for you to seek a particular personality in your master. Do not think of your master as being very remote from you, either. So many people do. He or she whom you will call master is a being who has freed him or her self from the bondage of human error and limitation. In other words, he or she is a master over all human limitations.

We speak sometimes of the Lodge of the Masters. We do not refer to a given building, a structure on the astral plane. We refer to a level of consciousness from which level all masters work. The master mind is one mind, and therefore there is no separation on that level of consciousness. All work in absolute harmony, and the motive of the work is to give forth wisdom, love and power to all creation of the earth. When a soul reaches a level or plane of consciousness in which it can comprehend the wisdom, love and power from the master, it naturally becomes at one with the master. There must be a point of contact, and if a soul is vibrating 'down here', it is missing the vibrations 'up there'. But when the soul has raised its consciousness to a higher level, then automatically it is in contact with the masters ... or with its own master. What does it matter? All are one.

People are accustomed to thinking of the master Jesus as the Master, but there are other souls who have evolved through earthly incarnations to the mastership. You, too, are half-way towards the same goal, and this is what you are all consciously or unconsciously working for. It is your destiny. There are degrees of mastership: we say degrees, but the actual meaning of the word is that it brings you to the one level of spiritual consciousness.

The great ones work under the guidance and stimulation of the Lord of the Sun, whom in your western world you worship as the Christ spirit. These great ones of the Christ Circle who descend to the earth, stimulate in people and in the earth itself this divine light. We would have you get a more universal idea of this force, this light, this life. You are so limited and cramped in your conceptions. You sincerely strive to realize this spiritual power, but it is at present like pouring a volume of pure water through a very small channel. Much of this life-force does not succeed in entering the human channel. It overflows, but it is never wasted, for it returns again in due course to the centre from which it flows. Thus there is a continual outpouring, continual return of this life, this light and power.

In summary, we wish that you might be very universal in your thought regarding the masters. Think of them as one, and when you have found that one you will see all, and in all you will see the one.

Who are the Masters?

When we speak of those whom you call masters, we know that you have many more questions. Are they very remote? Are you in contact with them? How many masters are there in the heavens?

We will answer that last question first. Their numbers are legion. Masters are those souls who have, through love and self-discipline, attained mastery over themselves. Because they have gained self-mastery, they have a degree of mastery over the elements, over physical matter. Having won a degree of freedom, they can live and manifest on more than one plane, in more than one place at a time. They are unlimited by time and space. This power within them has grown and has risen into the centres in the head and they have received divine illumination. Compared with the limitation under which the masses of humanity labour, they are free. Not all of them pass beyond the earth, for it is their joy to return sometimes to live in the physical body—or very nearly the physical body—in order to help the younger souls and those who need love and guidance. They walk by their side. They do not waste time or power, but live to serve God and human kind.

There are many, many such beings. They are messengers to humanity, and every one of you is entitled to receive communication from them. They do not wish to be worshipped. They are humble and gentle brethren. In the past ages, countless souls have withdrawn from mortal life to seek the glories of the spiritual state and to study and to learn self-discipline. They have learned the inner secrets of self-development, unfoldment of the self. They have learned the secrets of the awakening of the sleeping beauty of the soul. These secrets are sacred and cannot be forced.

They can only be discovered by the individual in the process of self-discipline, self-mastery, and through living the life as exemplified by Jesus the Christ, by the Lord Buddha, by the Lord Sri Krishna, Osiris, Mohammed, by all the world's great avatars, by the Indian masters and their disciples—the path of selfless, loving service; the path of humility and gentleness; the path of knowledge.

The final test, the final experience of the ascension of the master into the heavens is the withdrawal of the higher self from the denser life and the transmutation of the bodily atoms so that the tangible or the materialised body which the soul is using becomes permanent; but not in the earthly sense—in the heavenly sense. This is called the state of ascension, to which state all masters attain after the highest earthly initiation. The ascended master who has passed this high earth initiation whilst functioning in his or her physical body so transmutes its physical atoms into light that he or she is caught up, so that the body seems to fade behind a cloud from the sight of earth people. Although they appear to have withdrawn from the world, they still live and move and have their being in a higher form, such as the ordinary person cannot conceive. But they can still impress you with their presence.

Do not think that the heavenly hosts who draw close are unconcerned with all the things which trouble you—bodily, mentally, materially. Every secret of your souls is known to the masters. Those whom you call masters work as one mind. When they descend to the level of humanity, each has his or her particular work to do, perhaps along a certain line dealing with a certain aspect of truth. At the highest level all masters are as one, and the master mind is attuned, is complete in the Universal Mind—where truth abides at the heart or centre, and radiations of truth envelop the whole universe and every individual life. We want you to understand that among all the great masters there is complete harmony and at-one-ment. The voice of the one will speak through a number of voices and a number of individualities.

Let us also explain that the qualities of the Mother and the qualities of the Father dwell in all souls, and if a master chooses the body of a mother or a woman, it is for a purpose; if he chooses the body of a male that is also for a purpose, because of either the gentleness or the love of the mother or the power aspect of the father. There must be women masters (if you like to put it in that very crude earth language) as well as men masters. Try to think of the Brotherhood as a brotherhood of souls. When you can enter the Lodge above you will find that all within are just brethren, with no thought of gender.

Now, let us gaze upon the perfect form of an Elder Brother—a master. What is the impression made upon us as we gaze upon that perfect form? Oh, such gentleness, such sweetness, such love! Can you conceive the purity and loveliness of the master soul? Can you see the expression, shining with love—not weak or tepid—a love which can withhold as well as give? Now, hold this picture, my brethren ... feel the wisdom, the tenderness, the gentleness of the Mother, together with the strength, the power, the courage of the First Principle, the Father. See therefore the dual soul, and see this soul with power to watch over all human kind. Almost impossible as it is for the human mind to grasp, we would indeed endeavour to convey to you this sense of loving care in which you live and have your being.

Seeking the Master

We should like to speak to you on the topic, 'seeking the master'. We might have said 'seeking a master', bearing in mind that there are many beings called 'masters', many Wise Ones behind, serving all humanity. But we have chosen to say, 'seeking the master', in order to particularise, to stress your own master. Do you know that every man and woman has a master? Perhaps you are seeking the master, too: your particular master.

The man or woman on the outer plane will say, and with reason, 'But why talk about unknown masters? We cannot contact them. You tell us there are those who have actually met masters, and have received teaching from them. But we know nothing of this. How can we know that they exist?'.

Well, the remedy is in your own hands. You have the power to find your master for yourself, and can in due time actually meet and converse with him or her while you are still living in the physical body.

In the schools of the mysteries, both past and present, the injunction is always given to the neophyte, the young candidate: 'Go to your master, he or she will instruct you.' In the temples of old, the pupils were trained by their masters, they sought their master. The difference between now and then is that of old there were temples specially built for the purpose of spiritual training. You see their remnants scattered over the lands of Egypt and India. If you have visited them, you will be aware of the power which permeates the spot. You need not go to Egypt, however, or to India, since in your own abbeys and monasteries you may feel the sacredness, the power, the peace and harmony which permeates these places. It was here that the young candidates, the young priests, sojourned; and learned the wisdom of the ages from their masters.

To prevent confusion as to who your master is, let us explain that there is one master Mind, or one plane of conscious life which is known as 'the master'. You will find no fundamental difference between the teachings of the various masters, but each bears the hallmark of his or her status of life. He or she will be complete master of self, of emotions. He or she will have no fear, will know no sickness, will live to express the Father–Mother God in every act and word and thought.

No master, we repeat, will contradict another: masters do not give essentially different teaching. They do not vary; they speak always the same language: not the language of any one particular country, but the language of the spirit, the language of love.

One truth may be expressed through many masters. But, although they do not contradict the fundamentals, it may be that they bring through differing aspects, or one particular aspect, of the Deity, of the Godhead. One person may express great power; he or she may be vibrating on the power aspect of God; and may then be found as a ruler among people. We are not suggesting that those in your governments are masters!—rather that the power ray is one on which masters may work for the wellbeing and upliftment of humanity.

Another master, on the other hand, may vibrate to the ray of harmony, art and music. Yet another may vibrate on the ray of healing, and while possessing the other attributes of mastership, may be concentrating on healing humanity. If your interest lies there, then it is likely that your particular master will be on the healing ray. The master Buddha was vibrating on the wisdom ray entirely; and his pupils, or chelas, found mastership through wisdom, through contemplation, through withdrawing from the world, and following the intuition, or the wisdom of the stillness within.

The master Jesus, by contrast, was the prepared channel for the light of love. The Christ which manifested through Jesus is the Son of God. Do you understand? The love aspect of the deity manifested through Jesus in full degree, and found expression in action and service, thus supplanting the power aspect known to the Hebrews as Jehovah. The word Jehovah itself is a word of power.

You will find your master on the ray most harmonious to yourself. Leadership may be the ray upon which you are evolving; and through the power growing within you—not of domination over others, but the power to uplift and strengthen and inspire your brother or sister—you will find your master. If wisdom is your goal, the longing for wisdom and understanding, then you will meet him–her on this vibration. If, to you, Jesus Christ is the ideal, you will find Him, through following in His footsteps and doing exactly as the Christ within inspires you to do.

The very gentleness and meekness portrayed in the four Gospels brings to you a picture of Christ. If you would meet Him face to face, strive in all ways to do and think as He would do and think. He would be gentle, loving and compassionate, and have humility. *The Father that dwelleth in me, He doeth the works*: not I. You must attune yourself to the God life, and know that no thing in you is good except that which cometh from God. Do you feel this truth? .... *I and my Father are one.* The Christ, speaking through Jesus of Nazareth, was bringing through part of God ... the Christ, or the Son aspect of God.

Which among you does not long to meet the Master? How many feel that if only they had lived in the time of Jesus Christ, and had the opportunity of those who lived with the master Jesus, how much better they would be, how much greater their power for good! How much easier to follow Christ if we could but hear His voice!

Many look forward to the second coming of the Master, and think how changed everything will be when He reappears. This is no new idea ... the second coming. Do not think that the age of Aquarius, the age of brotherhood, is the first time that the condition of peace on earth, for which you hope, has prevailed. Life moves in cycles. There is nothing new, in the whole of creation. Life is rhythm, a breathing-in and a breathing-out; an inhalation and exhalation. What is today, was yesterday; what comes tomorrow, also came yesterday. As it was in the beginning, is now and ever shall be, world without end! Study that phrase from your Christian prayers; meditate upon it, and all manner of new thoughts will come: the veil will grow more transparent, and you will see the meaning of the future.

We seek the master, our master! For this brief moment let us forget all else. My master! Say it to yourself; close your eyes and say, 'My master.'. Do you form a picture of your master, or do you find it easier to visualize some picture of Jesus Christ and accept Him as your master?

Never mind which. It is sufficient that you have a master, and that you desire to know him–her ... to feel that intimate relationship ...to feel that you are immersed in the master's aura ... that he–she knows you, and understands every struggle of your life; sympathises with every failure; looks kindly upon you, and has sympathy with your limitations and your intense longing for greater spiritual realization. Your master knows you as no soul living on earth can know. He or she is part of you. Is this not a glorious thought?—inspiring, comforting, strengthening! Does power flow into your breast as you think thus? Of course! You feel your master's power permeating your being; you feel its stimulation, and your whole body begins to tingle and vibrate. The vibrations are caused by the thought of your master.

You hope to meet your master when you leave your physical body. Do not be too sure—if we can say this without upsetting you. Unless you can recognize your master here, begin to picture your master in your imagination, you may not do so in the astral body. You may meet, but you will not know him–her. You may meet your master tomorrow, of course, or even tonight; it is quite likely; but unless you have the ideal within your breast, you will not recognize him or her in another.

How will your master appear? Listen! Your master may speak to you through the lips of another, tonight or tomorrow. You must seek your master. He or she will not run after you and reveal him- or herself. Your master will not say, 'Lo, I am your master; follow me!'. No: it is for you to find him or her and then to follow. It may take a long time but you can certainly meet him or her face to face in this day of life; and your master can also speak to you through some book. You may hear and see him or her in some glorious sunset, or great piece of music, or in a lovely poem ... in the message of a bed of flowers or in a pine tree.

The Meeting Place

It may help you to know how you, as a simple brother, a simple sister, may hold communion with your master. All that your highest self creates in the human form; all that your highest self is capable of imagining your master to be like, so will you fashion into his or her form in your mind, and thus his or her presence will become a reality to you. It is a mistake to attempt to name or label the one who is your master. These Elder Brethren of the human race have withdrawn from the outer life to the silent places above the earth. Whilst there are certain members of the great Brotherhood who use physical bodies for the purpose of their work, there are others who work in the beyond, and only men and women who have developed a like beauty of character and love in their souls will be able to recognize any one of these, our Elder Brethren.

You see the vital necessity of daily striving to become gentle and Christlike. We always think that the beautiful gentleness of Jesus is the great ideal to follow. In this personification of the Christ Light, the Son of the Father–Mother God, we can all visualize our master. We have used the personification of Jesus as an illustration of what we mean, but from within your own breast you may create another personification of a gentle, loving son–daughter of God. You may—indeed it is more than likely that you will—meet the one who is your particular master, on a different vibration from that on which the master Jesus works. However, all that you can create in your mind of a beautiful, loving, gentle, pure and perfect man–woman, will enable you to meet your true master on the higher planes of consciousness. You may meet him–her on some great mountain height—there are many retreats in which the Elder Brethren of humanity dwell—but you may also expect to contact them in your heart first: through your higher self, your inner consciousness, your still small voice.

Remember this: you will find your master first in the secret chamber within your own heart, and when you have found him–her there, you will know the voice of your master, and he–she will reveal the way you should treat your brother and your sister on earth; how you should act in certain circumstances in your life. Your master says to you: 'Cast out fear ... be unafraid ... be whole ... know no desire'. And again: 'Be sincere to this woman or this man'. If your master's ideal in your heart makes you unwilling to stoop to the low and the mean and the petty, particularly in the things unseen or unknown; if you can act always as though your master is by your side, and do what you feel would be your master's way: then you are nearing the meeting-place, and will meet him or her face to face on earth. But you must know the master within first; you must know him–her in this way before you can hope to recognize your master manifested in a physical body. Yes! masters are walking the streets of your cities, and you will find them, if you seek.

Life is good; life is beautiful! Do not be jostled and hurried by fears. *The Prince of this world cometh, and hath nothing* in common with the master within. You must learn to know in your innermost being that there is nothing to fear. Be at peace, and seek, every moment of your life, the presentation of your master. He or she may already have spoken to you, without you recognizing. He or she may have spoken through some uninteresting man or woman you know. Masters do not blazon their qualities or advertise themselves. *Seek and ye shall find; knock and the door shall be opened unto you!*

Finding the Master Within

Carry the light of the master's love into the world. The whole of the Revelation of St John contains mystical teaching of the two aspects of life—the living and the dead; the true and the false; the real and the unreal; the spiritual and the material. Do not let the spiritual things be to you as fantasies. Let the spiritual truths become to you the realities of life. Live by the spirit, and see the growth and evolution of the spirit in earth, until the bonds of earth shall be broken, and materialism shall die and the spirits of the just and the true shall be caught up into the heart of God, and there shall be *a new heaven and a new earth.*

The Brotherhood in spirit would have you know that you must learn to distinguish between your true inner self and your outer physical life, because the inability to distinguish the one from the other is in itself responsible for much of the confusion which confronts you. You must develop your spiritual being surely, strongly and purposefully, every day of your life: first by the practice of meditation, and secondly through the continual practice of love in your daily life.

So we say that the very first thing to strive to do is to get your values right. Do not be confused between what is called material and what is called spiritual, but endeavour to live in the awareness of the presence and the power of the invisible to help you and to help all human kind along the path of evolution. The world appears to you to be chaotic. Humanity itself creates this chaos. Out of chaos, God creates beauty and perfection. You are the instrument of God and you can be and are being used to bring about a right state for all people. All we say is that you *cannot live by bread alone*, which means you cannot live by material standards; you must learn to look beyond, and recognize the sweetness of the Christ life, not only in good people, not only in the godly company, but in the brother or sister by your side.

Some of you still find cause to misjudge others. Strive to overcome intolerance. Try to put yourself in another's place and feel what they feel during their crucifixion (because that is what it can amount to). Above all, keep your values right, your vision pure, your heart full of love.

Contact with those whom you call 'master' is not often made on the astral plane, and there can be a misrepresentation of the masters from that astral plane. So it is necessary to train yourselves to become *en rapport* with the higher mental plane (which is above the astral), because it is at this level that you will in time come face-to-face with the Elder Brethren. You have to train yourselves first of all through meditation. We put meditation first for the reason that as you learn to meditate, you are learning to raise your consciousness above the astral plane to the higher mental. True meditation takes place on the higher mental plane, and as you practise meditation you become more and more able to fix your consciousness upon this plane and to distinguish it from the confusion of the astral.

Even so, how can you be sure that you are reaching that higher mental plane? Well, Jesus gave you the key when he said: *By their fruits ye shall know them*. One striking quality of the message coming from a high source is that of humility. You will never find a true teacher making big claims. A true teacher will understate rather than overstate. True teachers will be very careful about what they say, and you will always notice a quality of love, humility, gentleness, in their conversation.

Do you think that if some master or one of the Elder Brethren spoke to you in a public place, or sat beside you in a public vehicle, you would recognize them? In all probability, no. You see the desirability and the need to develop a quality which will enable you to recognize a master? We would have you realize that you have within yourself a centre of light and power; and you know that within you lies the opportunity to grow in spirit, to grow in stature until you, too, become as the Master, for did he not say, 'What I do, you will do also'?* We would hold this ideal ever before you.

You, the Master

It is difficult for anyone on earth to say he or she is a master. However, you have to attain the level of mastership through physical life. This is why we come back to try and help you reach understanding. Never make the excuse that you can't do it, or that your time has not come, or that it's all very well in the remote future. Keep the ideal before you.

This path is your path; and they who come to minister to you come with love and patience. Do not be cast down. It is good to recognize your shortcomings, for humility is a true companion of the aspirant on the path. Keep your feet on the earth, but lift your faces towards the heavens, for the light which floods into you from on high will steady your feet and guide them in the right path. Have confidence in this divine nebulous force that you do not understand and which you feel is very distant. This divine fire is within your very being, and as you raise your face to the sun, the rays of the sun stimulate this individual spark.

A beautiful and wonderful future awaits you all. You are all laying the foundations of that good, wholesome and happy future which we see is coming to humanity. Look around; and whenever you see some

---

*The reference is to John 14 : 12, quoted at the head of Chapter VIII

good impulse, some good impetus coming from a person, do not immediately say: 'I wonder what is at the back of it'. Hold fast to the good. If some leader of the nations puts forth an effort for peace or goodwill—even if he or she may not fully realize it and not be completely at one with others—help him or her by giving the right construction to this good impetus. We are saying this today about world affairs because from now on these good impulses will be put forth. Encourage them on the inner planes by believing good in any man or woman who is endeavouring to respond to the Christ impulse. *Am I my brother's keeper?* says your bible. Yes indeed! We are all our brother's keepers, whether still in the spirit life or on the earth. Many, many people are being pushed downhill by the good intentions of the so-called good. Too often self-righteous good intentions have caused bloodshed and brought suffering to humanity and also to the animal world. Truly good intentions come only from the simple, trusting, faithful heart.

The true brother or sister recognizes that every poor, fallen soul contains a spark of God which needs fanning into life. Alas, so many folk drive their brethren into the pit of darkness! The only salvation for the world is God-in-man, in-woman. You can choose to allow God to enter and use you to love and succour your companion beings—or allow the devil to come in to condemn and destroy. The path of the true brother or sister, aspiring to become a master soul, is quite clear.

The master soul, we repeat, is the gentle soul, the wise, loving and compassionate soul, patient in adversity, who never loses faith in God and the ministering angels of God. Our last word of advice is simply: Love thy neighbour and love thyself. Do good to them that hate you. Do good to your own soul, not thinking unduly about yourself but abiding by wise laws of right living, right eating, right thinking. Create as far as you can pure and right conditions in your home and surroundings. Remember the trials and the difficulties in another person's life which may make them irritable and sharp. Turn away wrath by gentleness and love, remembering that as you feel hurt and irritated, so may your companions feel too; and until you can feel with the feeling of your companions, you cannot be a master soul.

This, my friends, is the meaning of the old doctrine of the atonement, the at-one-ment. You see how it comes right into your human relationships every minute of the day. You cannot do it all at once, we know, but make a good try—beloved friends, make a good try, and as you raise yourselves, you will raise all people.

Would that we could find words with which to describe the glory of the form of the master soul. We can give you perhaps an inkling of that glory by describing the form as appearing like a jewel. Now, think of a jewel casket; then open your casket, and lying upon a soft cushion see a golden jewel flashing like fire, dazzlingly beautiful. Rays from this jewel go in all directions. From this try to get some idea of the glory of a master soul. Keep this ideal ever before you, remembering that you, in spite of your limitations and failures, are created to become that glorious jewel—some day. For as the bulb grows in the dark soil and eventually raises its head to the sunlight—a beautiful flower—so every human soul contains within its being potential qualities of becoming a master soul, a perfect jewel.

Standing by a lake (in the world of spirit) and watching the reflection of goodness and beauty, you can see your own reflection, and see yourself in comparison with God and God's manifestation of truth. And thus you gain the jewel of truth. It is then that the dewdrop shines within the lotus.

We have endeavoured to give you a picture of a master soul. This master soul is what you will become. So all your problems and difficulties, though very hard to bear at times, have a meaning and will prove worthwhile, because it is through enduring them with courage, faith and trust in the love and wisdom of your Creator that you will go forward towards that perfect state and the Golden City of God. More than this, you will be helping the whole of humanity onward to reach that state which has been called the golden age.

Service

A group of pilgrims were searching for a master, one who was said to have great wisdom, one who would help them to find heaven. In due course, after a long and troublesome journey, they found themselves before a cave in the mountainside, in which the one who was said to be a master was seated in meditation. After a time of preparation, they were invited to enter the presence of the holy man. He remained in meditation as they entered—no word was spoken. But when they were seated, he raised his face; and they saw shining, not only from his face, but from his whole being, a glorious light which penetrated their own beings, until they felt that their bodies and the very clothing they wore were alight, blazing, even as the light which they saw in the master's aura. They absorbed his beauty, and were bathed in the glory of the heavenly light.

This is a simple illustration of what it is expected that you, individually, will give to human kind as you unfold. It is hoped that one day you will become so impregnated with the holiness and love of the Master that you will carry His–Her gentleness and love out into the world. Is it asking too much? It is difficult for you, we know, for the world may appear cruel and hard, but it is peopled with a suffering humanity, and those who appear cruel and hard, as you would describe them, are truly in need of the light which you can carry them. Not only are you a vessel of light, even as a little lamp burning on the altar, but you may relight the lamp of your brother, your sister.

You cannot comprehend infinity nor eternity, but you can listen when we tell you that deep, deep within you, in the inner planes of consciousness, are worlds of indescribable and unbelievable perfection; and that, as you learn to command yourself, your emotions, your fears, your anxieties—as you learn to enter into the sanctuary of peace in preparation—you will, by your own freewill and power, advance into the glories of a world perfect in colour, harmony; a world of music, a world of goodness, a world where everything falls into its appointed place without hindrance. St John gave a description of the New Jerusalem, of the Golden City paved with gold, the gates decorated with blazing jewels. What is this but a portrayal of your own inner self?—your form the temple, your chakras the gates studded with beautiful jewels, your heart the throne upon which the King and Queen rest.

John, Soul of Humanity, we love you! May we follow whither you have led. May we gain deeper understanding! May all our brethren see beyond the veil, to that which awaits each and all: the perfect union of soul and spirit in the One who is their beloved!

INDEX

THE WHITE EAGLE PUBLISHING TRUST, which publishes and distributes the White Eagle teaching, is part of the wider work of the White Eagle Lodge, a meeting place or fraternity in which people may find a place for growth and understanding, and a place in which the teachings of White Eagle find practical expression. Here men and women may come to learn the reason for their life on earth and how to serve and live in harmony with the whole brotherhood of life, visible and invisible, in health and happiness. The White Eagle Publishing Trust website is at www.whiteaglepublishing.org.

Readers wishing to know more of the work of the White Eagle Lodge may write to the General Secretary, The White Eagle Lodge, New Lands, Brewells Lane, Liss, Hampshire, England GU33 7HY (tel. 01730 893300) or can call at The White Eagle Lodge, 9 St Mary Abbots Place, Kensington, London W8 6LS (tel. 020-7603 7914). In the Americas please write to The Church of the White Eagle Lodge, P. O. Box 930, Montgomery, Texas 77356 (tel. 936-597 5757), and in Australasia to The White Eagle Lodge (Australasia), P. O. Box 225, Maleny, Queensland 4552, Australia (tel. 07 5494 4397).

You can also visit our websites at

www.whiteagle.org (*worldwide*);
www.whiteaglelodge.org (*Americas*);
www.whiteeaglelodge.org.au (*Australasia*),

and you can email us at the addresses

enquiries@whiteagle.org (*worldwide*);
sjrc@whiteaglelodge.org (*Americas*); *and*
enquiries@whiteeaglelodge.org.au (*Australasia*).